I am Me

by

Patrick Dati

D1444793

Disclaimer:

This book is intended as a general guide to the topics discussed; it is not intended and should not be used as a substitute for professional advice. You should consult a competent doctor, therapist or licensed counselor with specific issues, challenges or questions you may have.

Although every precaution has been taken to verify the accuracy of the information contained herein, the author and publisher assume no responsibility for any errors or omissions. No liability is assumed for damages that may result for the use of the information contained within.

I wrote this book because I am a voice for all victims of abuse. I know the pain and sadness that comes from keeping secrets, of "not telling," of moving through life in the shadows so no one notices you. I know the despair that portends suicide attempts and the desperate and elaborate lies you tell yourself over and over again just so you can get out of bed in the morning. I was one of the 85% of all abuse victims who never speak of the unspeakable things they have endured.

But not anymore.

I hope my story will help others understand that not only can they survive their past and all its ugly repercussion, but how they can use it to become who they truly are. Although the path to releasing pain and choosing happiness is never easy, it starts with one simple commitment, one promise that never gets broken no matter what: Just be YOU.

Because after all, you are you and I am me. And that's as perfect as it gets.

Table of Contents

Prologue
Mentor

Sometimes I think my life is just chaos and suffering. Other times, I think nothing happens in my life out of order because I'm protected and guided by a God who loves me. I tend to think the former as I'm living my life in the moment. I think the latter when I reflect back on my life's journey many years later. As of this moment, I can say I have finally become the person I've yearned to be all my life. And I love the person I've become.

A couple of years ago, a former co-worker came back into my life quite unexpectedly. During a downtown commute to work one day, I noticed that the man sitting across from me on the train kept staring at me. I suspected he might have more than a passing interest in me, possibly checking me out. But, soon I learned there was something more to this stranger. When our train finally reached Chicago's downtown Loop, I realized that this was no stranger at all.

"Bob?" The moment I said his name, he recognized me too, and everything in my life changed.

We were both amazed and delighted to see each other again after so long. Several years ago, Bob and I had worked together at a company that developed training programs for insurance agents. I was in marketing, and he wrote the training programs. Bob was gay and had been 'out' for many years. But when we had worked together, I was still acting straight while secretly exploring gay life.

I had pictures of my daughter all over my desk at work, so I figured Bob had no idea that I was gay. I came out a couple of years later, after leaving the company.

When we met again on the train that day, I didn't reveal my secret to Bob because we were both too busy rushing off to work. There simply wasn't time for that kind of acknowledgment. But before we parted, Bob and I swapped phone numbers and told each other how much we'd like to get together.

I always knew Bob was gay because he never tried to hide it when we worked together. He had lived a life I had only dreamed of living. But like my life, Bob's earlier years were difficult, too. He had fallen in love with a boy who became his best friend when he was only ten or eleven years old. The boy was straight, so Bob could only love him as a friend. But that kind of love for a young, gay boy can be brutal. It involves constant hiding and, basically, living a lie. So when Bob turned seventeen, he joined the Air Force and left behind family and friends he believed would never accept him as a gay man.

Bob served four years in the Air Force and then, because nothing had changed in him or in his hometown, chose to enter a monastery to devote his life to God. Bob's own church had taught him that homosexuality was a sin. Therefore, he figured the only way he could live a life of integrity was to practice chastity while at the monastery. Bob also practiced poverty, obedience, and silence for seven years as part of his new calling.

In his fifth year as a monk, Bob was sent to university to study for a degree. One evening at the end of his second year, Bob finished studying and, rather than putting on his habit as he usually did, went out for a cup of coffee in a simple shirt and pair of slacks. While walking down the street, a close friend approached but then walked right past Bob, unable to recognize him out of his habit. The moment so shocked Bob, he had to stop and collect his thoughts for a few moments. In that instant, he woke to the realization that he was *hiding* instead of fully revealing himself to the world. Only then did he realize that he had only one life to live. Bob decided then and there to live life true to himself, no matter the consequences. He was terrified, but committed.

That night Bob wrote his superior to tell him of his decision to leave the monastery. A few weeks later, after signing all the necessary papers, he moved to Chicago without a penny in his pocket. Bob was walking into his new life with nothing but his determination to fully be himself for the first time in his life. He was twenty-nine years old and scared. A former monk Bob knew let him sleep on his couch until he got settled. Shortly thereafter he met a good man and fell in love with him. The two wound up sharing their lives for the next forty years until Bob's partner died in 2008.

Bob and I would become close friends over the two years following our chance reintroduction. Bob was trying to find his way through his grief for his lover. I was trying to find my way out of a false persona to my true self, and Bob became my mentor in this process. He encouraged me to love myself and to not be controlled by other people - particularly members of my own family. He'd say, "Just be yourself, Patrick. People will love you for who you are. They'll love you even more because they'll know *who* you are. Stop hiding like I did and be who you are."

Bob and I spent most evenings together talking about our lives. We developed a ritual for Sunday nights. I'd come over in the afternoon and we would drink. Then I'd make supper, sometimes inviting friends over.

But, I had become depressed because for the past two years I had been living with my mom and dad. I had moved back home after breaking up with my first partner, Bradley. I lived upstairs, my older brother Marco in the basement, and our parents on the first floor. My dad was dying of cancer and we were all focused on caring for him. Marco and I took turns changing his diapers and cleaning him. Dad preferred my help because I was gentle with him, while Marco was rough. My dad was embarrassed by the humiliation of having to be cared for like a baby, and he felt he was a burden on us. He wasn't a burden on me, though. I loved him, so it wasn't difficult for me. But the sadness of it all was painful. No matter how tough it got for us, though, we were all determined not to send Dad to a nursing home during his final days. Dad ultimately succumbed to his cancer in October 2010.

One Sunday night in February 2011, I had an awakening - an awakening like Bob had experienced more than forty years earlier. I had mine with Marco, my big brother and my bully. On this night, I was hanging out at Bob's house. We had had too much to drink, talking about our lives. I remember Bob saying, "Stop living your life to please your family. If they love you, they'll love you more if you just show them who you really are and *be* who you are. It may take time, but it will gradually, slowly happen. They'll love you because of who you really are. Just be who you are. You'll be fine."

While we were talking, my mom called and asked me when I was coming home. After humiliating me by saying she hoped I wasn't drinking too much again - which, of course, I was - she told me my nieces Jessica, Jo Ann and Sue were over playing cards with her and my brother, Marco. They had asked me to stop by the liquor store to buy some wine. I said I would but felt irritated since I was taking the bus home and stopping by the liquor store would be inconvenient for me. They all had cars and could easily drive the three blocks to the liquor store themselves, I figured.

After the call, I was anxious to be done with it, so I left Bob's and took the bus to the liquor store. I grabbed a couple bottles of wine and proceeded to the cashier to make the purchase. I didn't know the woman working at the counter, so I was aggravated when she asked me for my ID.

I told her, "I'm sorry, I don't have any ID on me, but I'm 47 years-old and have been buying liquor here for over twenty years."

She told me, "No ID, no liquor." I was so upset and angry I called her a 'bitch' and walked out of the store. I regretted calling her that the moment I said it, but I was so upset by the whole situation I really couldn't help myself.

I called Marco and asked him to come pick me up. I also told him that he'd have to buy the wine himself. He was angry because he had to leave the card game. But by the time Marco got to the store he was furious at me for reasons I couldn't understand. He ordered me into his truck and took my money for the wine. When he went into the store, I could see Marco talking to the woman I had insulted. It was obvious he was getting more upset by the minute.

When Marco got back in the truck, he started screaming at me. "You little bastard! Where the fuck do you get off going into my liquor store and calling a woman I know a bitch?" he bellowed.

I was so scared by the fury of his anger that I thought of jumping out of the truck and walking home. He didn't let up, continuing to scream at me even when we got home and entered the house. I ran upstairs to my room to hide but could hear Marco loudly telling my mom and nieces what had happened. His exaggerated tone had me coming off like a madman.

I knew I had to get out of the house. Marco was so angry at me that I thought he might beat me to death. I grabbed a backpack, threw some clothes in it, and went down to the kitchen to leave. Marco paused for a moment when I entered the kitchen, looking at mom and then me. Then he screamed, "Where do you think you're going you little bastard?"

I said, "I'm leaving this crazy house. I've had it with you and your abuse. I'm never going to take your abuse again!"

Enraged, Marco shouted, "You little faggot, I hate you! I've *always* hated you! Go, I want you gone. Don't ever come back. I'll kill you if you do."

I looked at him and said, "Thanks for finally saying what I've been waiting all my life for you to say. You've always felt this way. That's why you always bullied me and told Mom and Dad you were just trying to make a man of me."

Furious, Marco yelled, "Get out! Get out of here, you faggot, or I'll kill you now!"

I ran from the house in terror. I felt just as frightened then as I did after a terrifying experience I'd had in a department store as a young boy. I was afraid for my life, so scared that I actually soiled my pants. At the same time, I knew in my being that I was leaving my past life and my hidden self behind. I had finally heard the voice of my family and the normal world through Marco when he called me 'faggot'. I woke up, just like my friend Bob did decades earlier when his good friend walked by him on the street and didn't recognize him. Both Bob and I had finally woken up to our true selves.

Running from the house, I was leaving my past behind. I ran into something new, something that I'd never known before. I felt alone, lost and cold. But, I also felt strong. I called Bob and told him what had happened and that I needed to stay with him that night. He sensed my desperation and fear and told me to wait at the corner and he would come pick me up. It was a cold, February night and it was raining. I was wet, shivering and miserable. But, for the first time in my life, I was *myself*. That's how Bob found me, and that's how he took me in that night.

Chapter 1 (1973)
Tormentor

I showered at Bob's house, and afterwards we had a long talk. I was still exhausted and terrified. For some reason, I told Bob the terrible story of what happened to me one day when I was only nine years old. I had told him this story many times before, but now I told it differently. I also saw it differently; what had happened with Marco earlier that evening made me finally wake up and see events in a new light. This time I started my story on the morning *after*, not the morning of that dark day.

I remember being abruptly awakened that morning, in 1973, by my mom yelling up the stairs at my brother and me: "We're leaving for church in forty-five minutes. Get up and get dressed and ready to go!"

Mom did that every Sunday morning of my life, but that particular Sunday her voice jolted me awake. I felt terrified. Then, my brother Marco rolled over in his bed and stared at me threateningly saying, "Listen, dork, not a word to Mom and Dad about leaving without me yesterday."

The horror of it all came rushing back to me when he said that. I turned away from him, shut my eyes, and buried my face in my pillow, trying to make it all go away. Trying to find a way to make it not have happened. I was clutching my rosary and remember praying myself to sleep the night before, begging Mother Mary to 'please make it go away, please do something to make it not have happened.' I fell asleep pleading for it not to have happened.

But it did happen, on a snowy, winter Saturday in '73. I didn't know it when I woke up, but it was my last morning of innocence. After that day, nothing would ever be normal again, especially me.

That morning, Marco and I were hanging out at home, both bored because we had nothing to do. My mother was cleaning the house like she did every Saturday. I remember hearing the phone ring. Mom answered it and yelled up stairs, "Patrick, your cousin Tim is on the phone!" I ran down stairs, grabbed the phone, and asked Tim what he was up to. I was excited because my cousin Tim was always fun to play with, and, sure enough, Tim asked me over for a snowball fight. Instantly, my boredom vanished.

I told Tim that I'd call our friend Tommy and we'd both be right over. When I called Tommy, we agreed to meet at the end of the block in a few minutes. When I started to get dressed, my mother asked me where I was going.

"Over to Tim's house," I said. "We're going to have a snowball fight."

Mom said, "You are not crossing Belmont Avenue by yourself. Marco's going with you. I have to run to the store."

She made Marco come down stairs and told him, "Your brother is going over to Aunt Jessica's house to play with your cousin, Tim. You go with him and watch out for him, especially crossing Belmont."

"Mom, why do I have to watch him? Why me?" Marco protested. "I don't want to hang out with a bunch of babies."

Mom insisted, "You watch them. They're your brother and cousin. Watch them or I'll tell your father." That did it for Marco. Then mom yelled, "Be home by three!"

As we walked out the door, Marco slapped me on the back of my head and said, "You big baby."

When Tommy saw us coming, he ran to meet us. "Hi, guys!" he shouted.

Marco, feeling the need to flex some authority, said, "Look, you little dorks, you need to listen to *me* today. I'm in charge. Whatever I say goes." Tommy and I traded a telling look, knowing we could con Marco into playing with us and having fun.

When we got to my Aunt Jessica's house, Tim started whipping snow balls at us from his hiding place in the bushes. Of course, we started flinging them right back at him. We were laughing and having a great time, until I started succumbing to the cold. I was covered in snow and shivering. I asked Tim if we could go into his house to get warm. But Tim said we couldn't because his parents went grocery shopping, and he wasn't allowed to have anyone in the house while his parents were away.

That's when Tommy said, "Let's walk down to Goldblatt's and buy some candy. We can hang out there and warm up."

Marco thought that idea was okay and asked, "Do you brats have any money?" We all dug into our pockets and pulled out our change. Altogether, we had about a dollar fifty -- enough! We ran down the block and into the revolving door of the huge Goldblatt's department store on the Belmont-Cragin block. We ran past the women's shoe department and into the heart of the store where the candy department was located. We were covered in snow, and it was dripping all over the floor. But, we were warm, so we were happy. After we made our purchase, we headed to the stairwell in the back of the store to gobble down our candy. As we were joking around in the stairwell, Tommy suggested a game of hide-and-seek in the store. Marco loved the idea and said, "Sure, this way we can stay warm, and we don't have to go back out into that snow storm."

As usual, I got to be the first 'seeker' in the game and they all got to hide. I turned into the corner of the stairwell and started counting. It was dark in the stairwell, and because I was suddenly alone, I started to get a little scared. When I got to 'ten', I took off on my hunt. It was Saturday so the department store was filled with shoppers. I annoyed a saleslady in the girls' clothing department by messing up the clothes racks looking for my buddies. The fact that I was all wet and my face was smeared with chocolate didn't help either. The look the saleslady gave me made me anxious. My anxiety would only get worse because I couldn't find the guys and hated being alone in large crowds of people.

Then, I suddenly felt the urge to use the bathroom. I think it might've been all the chocolate I had just eaten. I asked a cashier where the bathroom was and she directed me up the stairs and to the left. The thought of climbing the stair-well made me feel panicky; so much so that I thought of running all five blocks home to use our bathroom instead. I knew I wouldn't make it, though. Another thing I remember was my mom telling me I was not allowed to use a public bathroom unless I was with my brothers or my dad. There really wasn't much I could do, though, because I couldn't find Marco, and this just couldn't wait.

Bracing myself, I slowly hiked up the staircase, holding back the urge to relieve myself. I was frightened, and the staircase was dark and damp, with a strong bleach-like odor to it. When I got to the top of the stairs, I entered the men's room, which reeked of urine. There were five toilet stalls, one occupied. I entered one of the four empty stalls, took off my jacket, wiped the urine off the toilet seat with toilet paper, and went about my business.

After I had relieved myself, I heard the person in the stall next to me get up, leave the stall, and walk towards the door. I thought it odd that he didn't wash his hands first. Then I heard a 'click'. I realized this man had locked the bathroom door and was walking back to the stall next to me. Suddenly, my stomach dropped, flooding me with fear and panic. At that moment, I could sense my mom saying, *"Don't go into a public bathroom alone, Patrick."*

I then noticed that the inside of my stall was covered with pornographic images. Sketches of men's genitals alongside messages I didn't understand but sensed were malicious. Many of these messages had phone numbers and 'best time to call' notes written down. All at once, I noticed a golf ball-sized hole in my stall wall and caught the eye of the man in the next stall peeking at me through the hole for an instant before pulling away. I panicked, and as I wiped myself, I heard the man groan. I pulled up my pants and reached for my jacket. Then, the door of my stall burst open and a large, hairy man lunged towards me. I momentarily stopped breathing and froze.

The man pulled me out of the stall by my shirt and warned, "Don't say a word. Just do as I say. Follow me out the back door of the store and to my car. If you don't get in my car, if you run or scream or make any noise at all, I'll kill you. Do you understand?"

I started to cry. As the man pulled me towards the door I tried to fight him off. He told me, "Listen you little bastard, I'm not playing games. You're coming with me!"

He unlocked the door and tried to pull me with him, but I fought him with all my strength, trying to break free of his hold. Realizing I wasn't going quietly, he pushed me so hard I fell on the floor and he locked the door again. Then he unbuckled his belt and let his pants and underwear drop to the floor. He started fondling his penis. He was a huge, ugly man and he stank. I was paralyzed by fear and terror.

I don't think I could have screamed at the time but when I opened my mouth to try, the man covered it with his hand, leaning down to whisper in my ear, "One word, one sound, and I'll kill you." I started crying and shaking. He then pulled out a pocket knife and held it to my neck and repeated, "If you scream or make one more sound, I swear I'll kill you."

I fought to break loose when he grabbed me, but he was too strong. He pushed me to the floor next to the toilet. He covered my nose and mouth with one hand while the other ripped at the buckle of my pants and unzipped my fly. I was so scared I thought I was going to pass out. He pulled my pants off and pushed my face into the toilet. Then he started trying to force himself into my rectum. I twisted and fell to the floor under the toilet. He then pushed my head into the tile and proceeded to rape me.

The man warned, "You make one sound and I'll bash your head in." I cried, sobbing helplessly. I lay half-naked on the floor, shaking and terrified by what was happening to me. Finally, he groaned and climaxed inside me. I pulled my arms over my head thinking he was then going to kill me. Instead, he pulled his pants up and said, "Don't forget, one word and I'll kill you. I know where you live." He unlocked the bathroom door and escaped down the stairs.

I grabbed the toilet seat with both hands and slowly pulled myself up. My nose was bleeding from being ground into the bathroom tile. I clutched my jacket and stood against the wall. I was afraid to leave, thinking the man might be waiting for me at the bottom of the stair well. Just then, someone else walked into the bathroom and entered the stall my attacker had just been in. That prompted me to action. I bolted out of the stall, ran down the stairs and burst out the back door of the department store. I ran frantically through the store's rear parking lot, stumbling anxiously between rows of cars, terrified my attacker lay in wait for me there.

The snow was coming down heavily now. I was numb to the cold as I attempted to outrun my fear and horror over what had just happened. My jacket was still wide open and my clothes were soiled. I felt certain at that moment that the man was following me through the parking lot. I kept looking back for him as I ran and ran. I could feel my heart pounding, the tears streaming down my face, the fear gripping me from within. I just kept running through the snow and never looked back.

When I got home the house was empty. I ran upstairs to my bedroom and hid in the closet. I wrapped my arms around my knees and tried to stop shaking. I couldn't stop crying. I had never felt so alone.

Later, I heard the back door open and my brother Marco

screaming my name. "Where are you, Patrick? I'm going to beat your ass!" he snarled.

When Marco came into our room, he heard me crying in the closet. He opened the door and said, "What the fuck were you thinking leaving the store without me?"

Then he grabbed me, pulled me up, and punched me in the stomach and slapped me across the face. He yelled, "I'll give you something to cry about, you big baby." Marco pulled me up and punched me again, then threw me to floor. He said, "If you breathe a word of this to Mom and Dad, I'll kick your ass, again. Dork!"

I lay there on the bedroom floor in pain, wanting to die, wanting to be anyone or anywhere else at that moment. At the same time, I knew I had to clean myself up before Mom and Dad got home. I didn't want them to know what happened. I didn't want anybody to know.

Actually, I did consider telling Mom and Dad. I'd tell them I had disobeyed them and gone into the department store bathroom by myself. Then, I'd tell them what that man had done to me and what he had said. The second I thought that though, I knew I wouldn't tell them - or anyone - ever. The man had warned, *"If you tell, I'll kill you. I know where you live."* And I believed him.

I worried Mom and Dad might blame me for going into a public bathroom by myself. Did I deserve what happened? Was it my fault? Had I done something to invite this attack upon me? I knew Mom and Dad would punish Marco if I told them what happened – he was supposed to be watching out for me. I also knew Marco would beat me up afterwards for telling on him. I figured that's what Marco did while I was growing up: he watched me and he beat me, pretty much in equal measure.

I then went to the bathroom, took my clothes off, and stood under the warm water of the shower, washing my body over and over. I would have bathed forever if Marco hadn't banged on the door and yelled at me to get out of the bathroom so he could use it. As I left the bathroom, he sneered, "You're *worse* than a little girl."

After showering, I remember going to my bedroom and changing into my pajamas. I compulsively grabbed my rosary from the desk. Then I climbed into bed and pulled the covers over my head. I said the rosary, stopping every few minutes to beg God to forgive me for what had just happened to me. I couldn't stop praying as I found the repetition comforting. I kept praying until I heard my parents come in and yell for Marco to come help them carry groceries in from the car.

I heard my mom ask Marco where I was and Marco replying, "He's up in his bedroom, acting like a baby." Mom asked Marco if we had been fighting and he said, "No, he's just acting like a dork." I heard Mom fiddling with pans in the kitchen and, about an hour later, smelled the pungent yet pleasing scent of beef soup simmering on the stovetop. Minutes later, she called me to come set the table.

Wearily, I dragged myself out of bed and went downstairs into the kitchen. Mom looked at me and asked me why I was in my pajamas already. I told her I didn't feel good. She asked me to come to her and felt my forehead to see if I had a fever.

"No fever, what's wrong?" Mom asked.

I lied, "I have a stomach ache."

"You were eating candy with your cousin, weren't you?" she said.

I admitted I had, and she told me, "Go lay down until we're ready for dinner. I'll have your sisters set the table." I told her I didn't feel like eating dinner and she said, "You need to eat something. Now, go lay down."

At five o'clock, Mom called us to the table for dinner. I sat at my place and we all held hands and said Grace, with Dad leading the prayer. As we began to eat, Mom asked Marco about our afternoon.

Marco said, "We had a snowball fight and then we came home." Mom asked me if I got into a fight with my cousin. I told her, "No, we just hung out for a while."

My oldest brother, Michael, told us about a girl he met at school and liked. My sisters, Gabriella and Maria, giggled and asked her name. Michael said, "Her name is Betty, and you don't know her."

I then asked my father, "Can I be excused from the table?"

Dad said, "No, Patrick, you haven't finished your dinner."

Mom looked at Dad and said, "Butch, it's okay, let him go. He's not feeling well." Dad told me to go lay down in the living room and turn on the TV.

As I was leaving the room Marco told Dad, "You treat him like a baby. He's a big sissy."

Dad scolded, "You better watch your mouth. He's your little brother and I don't want you talking about him that way." My sisters started laughing, because Marco was always getting in trouble with our parents.

When dinner was over my sisters cleaned the table, and then everyone joined me in the family room to watch television. About an hour later, I asked if I could go to bed.

Mom said, "Honey, it's only 7 o'clock. You never go to bed this early on a Saturday night." I told her I just didn't feel well, and that I was tired.

"Go ahead," she said. "But we have to be up at 7am to get ready for church."

That night I lay in bed under the covers crying and dreading my life. When I heard Marco come in, I pretended to be asleep. I finally did fall asleep clutching my rosary in my hands and trying to remember what it felt like that morning to be me.

That was my last day of innocence as a boy. That terrible experience altered something inside me and would color every remaining day of my life. I didn't speak about it to anyone for over thirty-five years. It was my dark secret and I kept it festering within for many years to come.

Chapter 2 (1973 – 1978)
Learning to Hide

It seems incredible to me that, the next morning after church, we went home to a typical Sunday at my house. When Mom told us our Aunt Jessica and Uncle John and the kids were coming over for lunch, my brothers and sisters got excited as they usually did. What amazed me was that I did too, as if the previous day hadn't really happened. Maybe this would be how I'd cope with the attack, I figured.

Whenever we got together with my uncle and aunt and their kids, we were one, big happy family. Their kids were our ages, and they were our best friends. I loved my cousin Tim. We were born three weeks apart, so we pretty much grew up together. We did everything together. We even went to the same school.

In the afternoon, while Tim and I were in the basement playing with our Tonka trucks before lunch, I had to use the bathroom. I ran upstairs and, when I reached the bathroom, for some reason, everything from that day in the Goldblatt's bathroom came rushing back to me in vivid detail and emotion – I could see, even smell it all again. I started crying and shaking. I panicked and ran up to my bedroom. I grabbed my rosary and fell sobbing onto my bed.

My mother saw me run up the stairs and could tell something was wrong. She came up to my room a few minutes later and sat next to me on my bed. She said, "Honey, what's wrong? Did one of the kids pick on you?"

I said, "No mom, I just feel like being alone. It'll be okay. I'm not a baby."

Mom hugged me and said, "Patrick, you'll *always* be my baby, no matter how old you are."

I said, "Mom, please," and then she left me alone and went downstairs. I lay in bed reliving my Goldblatt's experience while squeezing my eyes shut and clutching my rosary as tightly as I could. I again begged God to make it all go away. But I couldn't make it go away. And, neither could God. It was all there, inside me; a nightmare from which I could not awaken.

After that weekend, I couldn't concentrate in school. As teachers talked, I'd either be reliving my awful experience or begging God to make it go away. My grades plummeted.

My ordinary, day-to-day life became a nightmare. I remember one Saturday afternoon my mom took me shopping with her. When she pulled the car into Goldblatt's parking lot, I was shocked. I had avoided the store ever since the rape. Panicking, I pleaded with my mom to let me wait in the car.

"No, Patrick," she chided. "Don't be ridiculous. You're coming in the store with me."

I was terrified. As before, every moment of the attack came rushing back to me all at once. I was again re-living my trauma, and I was out of my wits with fear. But, Mom forced me to go inside with her. As we walked towards the entrance, she grabbed my hand and opened the door.

Mom felt me shaking and looked at me with concern. She then asked, "What's the matter? Why are you shaking, honey?"

I told her I was afraid. She said, "Afraid of *what*, silly? Come on, I'm with you. There's nothing to be afraid of. I won't let anything happen to you."

I shut my eyes and just let her lead me through the store. I thought the man might be there, hiding somewhere. He might see me and my mom and kill us both.

When we got home, I ran up to my room, grabbed my prayer book and rosary and just held on for dear life. After that day, I began slipping the beads in my pocket daily and taking them to school with me. They had become a part of me, a comforting compulsion. Whenever I would start to feel depressed about the rape, I would say the rosary and hold my prayer book tightly. These were the only things that seemed to offer any real solace, to help ease this enormous weight on my shoulders.

My grades continued dropping because I couldn't concentrate. My spring report card showed I was failing every subject. My parents were so upset they hired a tutor to help me, without results. When school ended in June, the principal told my parents I was being held back and would have to repeat the third grade.

Nothing like this had ever happened to me before. I had never disappointed my parents, and they had always been proud of me. I was upset and ashamed. I felt haunted by my memories, burdened by my guilt and by the strain of keeping it all a secret.

My cousin Tim was going on to the fourth grade without me. I started to feel very isolated and my self-esteem plummeted. I started doing extra chores around the house thinking that if I pleased my parents in some other way they would love me as much as they loved me 'before' - before I failed a grade, before I disappointed them, before I was raped.

In desperation, my parents enrolled me in St. Ferdinand's Grammar School in Chicago the next semester. They figured that putting me in a private Catholic school would help improve my grades. I was actually happy to change schools and be with kids who wouldn't know I had flunked third grade. I was also happy that I could attend Mass every day and become closer to God. I hoped that He'd forgive me for my traumatic experience and somehow cleanse me of this dreadful memory.

St. Ferdinand's was wonderful for me. Because I was repeating a number of classes from my previous placement, the material seemed easier and my grades started to improve. I took a religion class and got an 'A' in it on my first report card. I felt safe enough in my church that I started making new friends.

My parents were thrilled because I seemed like my old self. They were proud of me once again. Unfortunately, this development only widened the gap between me and my brothers and sisters, who'd already felt I was favored simply by being the youngest. My siblings were all in public school, and resented me for going to a private, Catholic school. To them, it seemed like our parents just loved me more.

I amazed my Dad and brothers when I joined my school's football team. What they didn't know was that I joined the team to make *them* happy. After the rape, that's what I did - I tried to please everyone so they would like and approve of me. I hid the real me and started acting out a new role, one I created solely to win others' approval. But because of the rape – and another secret

– I believed in my heart that I wasn't fully worthy of that love and acceptance.

Joining the football team also gave me an opportunity to become friends with boys for whom I'd found myself attracted. I sensed what those feelings meant, but I buried the thoughts deep down within. They went against everything my family stood for, particularly our Catholic faith. These hidden feelings of attraction scared me, but they were a part of me all the same. Frankly, I didn't even care about football, and I really wasn't good at it. Nevertheless, I was happy playing football because my family came to all my games and cheered me on. And it was the first time I ever really got along with my brother Marco.

Looking back, I think Marco always sensed I might be gay, and perhaps he bullied me to 'make a man' out of me. He routinely called me 'sissy' or 'baby' while demanding I 'stop acting like a girl.' Marco wanted me to act like *he* acted. Of course, I couldn't.

The beatings from Marco were always more than just "boys being boys." That was how my parents described them to doctors whenever my injuries were severe enough to warrant a trip to the Emergency Room. With no real protection from my parents, I lived in constant fear because I never knew when Marco would next take out his rage and resentment on me.

My earliest memory of Marco beating me was when I was five years old. Marco was eating lunch as my mother gave me my bronchitis medication. She kissed my forehead and told me she loved me. When she left to start a load of laundry, Marco looked at me and told me he hated me. He then grabbed the back of my head and slammed me into the corner of the kitchen table, before running upstairs to his bedroom. I screamed and held my head as blood ran down my face. My mother came running back in and loudly demanded Marco tell her what had just happened.

Marco said, "I have no idea. I was upstairs in my bedroom and heard 'the baby' crying. He probably fell off the chair onto the table."

My mom called my dad, who was in the backyard, to inform him they needed to take me to the ER right away.

A couple years later, when I was seven, Marco and I were alone in the family room watching television. My parents had just come back from grocery shopping and my father told Marco to come out to the car and help carry the bags into the kitchen.

Marco complained, "Why don't you ask Patrick to help?"

Mom replied, "Do as your father asked or you're grounded."

When Marco returned from carrying in the groceries, he immediately started punching me. As I tried to get away from him, Marco pushed me head-first into the coffee table. My lip and mouth began bleeding and I started to cry. Marco ran outside into the back yard. My father grabbed a towel to wipe the blood from my face and once again rushed me to the ER.

As the doctor stitched up my mouth he asked my dad, "What happened to your son?" My dad told him, "My boys were fighting. You know how boys will be boys."

When we got home my father yelled for Marco to come to the kitchen. When he came into the room my father said, "Look what you did to your little brother!"

Dad started to whip Marco with his belt. After he finished, Marco ran up to our room. When I got into bed that night, Marco placed my pillow over my head and started punching me in the stomach. He told me if I said anything he would kill me.

On another occasion, when I was nine years old, Marco was teasing me at the dinner table, much to the amusement of our sisters. My father responded by grounding Marco for his behavior and ordered him to apologize to me. Marco apologized at the table, but when I got up to our room he pounced on me again. He threw me across the room so hard that I landed on my head. Shortly after that, I was dizzy and began to vomit.

Mom came in and asked, "Baby, are you sick?" I was so afraid of Marco that I lied and told her I'd fallen and hit my head. Once again my Mom and Dad had to take me to the Emergency Room, where the doctors diagnosed me with a concussion – the first of many I would receive from my brother Marco.

*****

When I was in the seventh grade, I became friends with a boy named Jeffrey. He lived on the next block from us and we went to St. Ferdinand's together. During the summer, we hung out, rode our bikes, and went to movies together, just having fun. We were inseparable. I liked him, and he obviously liked me. I also felt sorry for him because none of the other kids seemed to like him very much.

When I entered the eighth grade, I became one of the 'big guys' on campus. I was good-looking, well-built, and charming. Practically everybody seemed to like me, and I had worked diligently to create that effect with people. It's what I wanted most: to be liked, to be loved.

One day when Jeff and I were walking home from school, a couple of the school bullies followed us. One of the boys named Mike called Jeff a 'fag' and started to tease him maliciously. At one point, Mike turned on me and said, "Hey Dati, you must be a fag too, because you like Jeff so much."

That remark upset me and when I got home my mom sensed it and asked me what was wrong. When I told her it was nothing, she became upset and said, "Look young man, I want an answer, now. What's going on?"

I told her, "It's no big deal, Mom. Mike was picking on me and Jeff."

She replied, "I know Mike's mother through Girl Scouts. I'll speak to her about it."

I said, "Please Mom, don't. I can handle it myself."

As I walked up to our room, my brother Marco, who had been listening to us, followed me. He grabbed my arm and said, "I just heard what you told Mom about being picked on by Mike."

I told Marco I could handle it, but he said, "Tomorrow after school, I'm going to follow you. If Mike follows you again and makes any cracks, you kick his ass."

I refused. "No, I'm not going to kick his ass. I've never even been in a fight."

"You have two choices," Marco told me. "One: you kick the shit out of Mike. Two: I kick the shit out of *you*." The thought of another beating from Marco terrified me enough to accept his challenge. I resolved to confront Mike the next day.

As luck would have it, Mike followed Jeff and me home from school the next day, making wisecracks about us along the way. Marco was trailing just behind him. I knew I had to follow through on Marco's dare or I'd pay the consequences once I got home. Mike was calling us 'fags' and I don't know whether it was more fear or frustration that made me do it, but I turned around, jumped Mike, and just kept punching him until he begged me to stop. My friend Jeff was so terrified by all this, that he ran all the way home. And when I finally let Mike up, he ran home, too.

Beaming, Marco grabbed my arm, lifted it up like I'd won a boxing title, and said, "Brother, I've never been so proud of you!" Marco was so happy and proud that he couldn't stop talking about the incident even when we got home. Mom wasn't impressed, though.

"What kind of a person are you, Patrick, to beat up another person?" she asked. "We haven't raised you to act like that."

Lying, I told her, "I just couldn't take the abuse anymore, Mom." Of course, I didn't tell her that I'd taken on Mike simply to keep Marco from abusing me again.

After that incident, I started to distance myself from Jeff. Everyone at school found out about the fight and thought I was a hero for beating up Mike. To capitalize on my peers' new admiration, I started acting more masculine.

I also started eyeing Jeff with more suspicion. I noticed he had little interest in girls, and I became more acutely aware of his feminine qualities. Eventually, I avoided him altogether and stopped calling him. I did this because I was afraid, afraid of how much I actually liked him. I didn't want anyone to realize that what was in him was also in me. So, I hid and protected myself.

I joined in with the others at school, the 'normal' kids. I called Jeff a 'queer' one day and I could tell it hurt him - hearing someone he loved and trusted, a friend, calling him a queer. When I called him a queer I knew in my heart I had become one of 'them' - I had become a *bully*. After that, I just sunk deeper into the mire and hid as just another one of the 'normal' kids. I hung out with them, even spent time in their homes, and they and their families seemed to like me.

But I was moving into a dark place and I found myself deeper and deeper in the closet. I felt I had to hide who I really was at all cost. I wanted desperately to fit in with the normal crowd. I wanted to hide my real self just like I hid my childhood trauma. I felt about boys the same way Jeff felt about boys, and it scared me. It scared me the way the rape scared me.

There was another reason I wanted to break off my friendship with Jeff. It concerned that other secret of my heart. His name was Joey, and he was a friend of my brother, Marco. If Jeff was my good friend, Joey was my secret lover. He was Italian, muscular, and handsome. I thought he was beautiful, and I wanted him, desired him. But I hadn't a clue on what to do about it. I just liked looking at Joey, and I liked the feeling I got when I looked at him. I wanted to touch him, smell him, hold him, and kiss him. I wanted to sleep with him. I knew all this desire was forbidden and that I had to keep it a secret. And I did keep it a secret, just like the rape - it was that kind of secret. Something inside told me these feelings were wrong and if those I loved knew, they wouldn't love me anymore.

Marco and Joey used to play basketball all the time in the drive way, and I would watch them from my bedroom window. I'd get butterflies in my stomach from watching Joey. Whenever that happened, I would run to my night stand, grab my prayer book and rosary, and start praying. I loved Joey, but because of the bullies in my life, I convinced myself this emotion was wrong. I would never tell anyone how I'd felt about him. I would never tell anyone I was raped in the Goldblatt's men's room, either. I was fourteen and already stocking up on deep secrets. All I wanted was to be the normal kid my parents and siblings thought I was so they would love me and be proud of me. I loved pleasing my family. I'd do anything to make them love me, even if that meant hiding my true self and playing out a contrived role, just the way all the bullies in my life wanted me to act.

Then, one day, I again saw the man who raped me. It happened one Thursday afternoon in the winter of my freshman year. My friend, Tommy, asked me to hang out after school over at his house. I loved hanging out at Tommy's house because he had moved the year before to a new area of the northwest side of Chicago. Tommy's dad was a cop and he had wanted to get out of our old neighborhood and move their family into a nicer one. Tommy's parents always bought the newest electronics, and they had a TV with a VCR so we could watch movies whenever we wanted.

We were hanging out watching some scary horror film around four o'clock in the afternoon when we heard sirens and saw flashing lights on the block just across from Tommy's house. The police had the entire area blocked off. All of a sudden the phone rang; it was Tommy's dad calling from the police station. After Tommy's mom hung up the phone, she came into the family room and turned off our movie so we could watch the news instead.

Tommy asked, "Mom, what's going on outside?"

"Your father just called from the police station," she told us. "The police are searching a neighbor's house. Something about a murder." We all sat and watched the news coverage. It was really interesting because, as we watched the news, we also could peer out the window and see these very reporters covering the story.

Tommy asked, "Mom, can we go outside and see what's going on? Maybe we can get on the news. That would be so cool."

I agreed with Tommy, but his mom said, "Your father said no one is to leave the house, so stay put."

We had no idea what was going on. We just thought it was really cool that it was all happening right outside Tommy's house. A few minutes later, the phone rang again. This time it was my mother. After a moment, I could tell Tommy's mom was nervous from their conversation. Then, his mom called me into the kitchen and said my mother wanted to speak with me.

Mom said, "Tommy's mom assured me that you boys would not leave the house and that you're safe. Patrick, you listen to his mother and do exactly what she tells you. Your father and I will pick you up first thing in the morning."

I told her I was fine. "We're having fun watching the news and all the police outside."

She begged me, "Patrick, please don't leave their house!"

I said, "Alright Mom, whatever you say."

Tommy and I continued to watch TV. The news reporter started telling the story of a man who dressed like a clown at kids' birthday parties and who had also murdered young men and buried them under his house. We were amazed that this killer could be living on the block next to Tommy's house. Then, the newsman announced the killer's name: John Wayne Gacy. Next, they showed his picture. I froze, terrified. It was *him*, the man who raped me five years earlier.

I remember trying to act normal and then heading to the bathroom. But when I stepped into the bathroom, I broke out in a cold sweat and started shaking and crying. I put my hands over my mouth so Tommy and his mom wouldn't hear me. I sat down on the toilet and covered my face with my hands and tried to control my emotions. I splashed my face with water and composed myself so I wouldn't spin out of control in front of Tommy and his family. When I returned to the family room I said to Tommy's mom, "I think I should go home now."

She said, "Patrick, why, what's wrong? You're white as a ghost. Are you okay?"

I said, "I'm not feeling well, and I want to go home."

She said, "Honey, I would be happy to take you home but all the streets are blocked off and your mother told me to make sure you boys stayed inside. Listen to me, you boys go down stairs, away from the news and what's going on outside, and just play pool. I'll bring down some snacks, okay?"

Tommy chimed in, "Come on, bud, let's go down and get away from this craziness."

I wanted to go home bad, but I did feel safe in Tommy's home - - maybe it was because Tommy's dad was a cop and I knew he would protect us. I also had this overwhelming need to act natural and in control of myself. But *inside* I felt like I was unraveling, unable to fathom and cope with what I had just seen and heard on the news. So, I did what I was becoming a master at; I hid inside myself and acted normal outside myself.

After that day, I was overwhelmed with guilt. I kept thinking that if I had reported the rape and told my family, the police might have caught this monster and maybe many of those boys would not have died. The guilt I felt was so depressing and oppressive I even tried to kill myself.

About a week later, I went down into the basement of our home, drank a bottle of vodka, and swallowed a bottle of pills I found in the medicine cabinet. If my sister hadn't found me and called 911, I wouldn't be writing this today.

Chapter 3 (1983 – 1987)
Jacob, Stella & Me

After high school, I started my freshman year at Columbia College with a dream of becoming a news reporter or anchor for a major television station. Columbia College had a good reputation, and it was close to home. Even if I didn't want to stay in Chicago, I was skeptical whether my parents would allow me to go out of state. Columbia seemed like a good choice for me at the time.

My parents had a difficult time paying my Catholic school tuition, so I was reluctant to ask them to pay my college tuition, also. My dad told me not to worry about tuition. All that was important to him was that I finish college and create a life for myself that would make him proud. I loved him, so I made myself want what *he* wanted. As always, I was living out my parents' dream for me.

I started at Columbia in September of 1983. I was anxious to be with other students who wanted the same things in life that I felt I did. The students at Columbia were very different from those at the Catholic school I had attended, though. I'd gone from a highly regimented and uniformed school environment to one where everyone freely expressed their individuality. I had never been around people who expressed themselves so openly, who said what was on their minds, and dressed to express their individuality. Columbia students amazed me, even though, like me, most of them seemed to hail from simple, blue collar families.

I wanted a good education. I wanted to be rich and successful, and I wanted to meet different kinds of people. Mostly, I wanted to meet people like the ones I'd met at Columbia; students with a passion for being themselves. I made friends quickly, and I started to live vicariously through them. At home I continued to be the model son my parents wanted me to be. But at college, I explored life through the lives of my new friends. I watched them and wondered if I, too, could express myself as they did, as a true individual. I knew I was a long way from realizing this goal. I really didn't have a clue how to just be myself. I could still only see myself as an extension of my large, Catholic family. To say I was confused would be a serious understatement.

My first semester in college was a joy for me, though. My new friends were so different from the kids I grew up with. Some were punk rockers with piercings and tattoos all over their bodies. Most of them had dyed their hair bold, unnatural colors. And they all tended to dress in creative, unusual ways.

Even though I was getting good grades and working hard, my parents worried about me because of my new friends. My dad wanted me to leave Chicago and go to school in another city. His uncle Vito lived in Las Vegas and was successful, so my dad thought I should go to college there. During spring break, Dad told me that he and Mom had a surprise for me. They were taking me to visit the University of Nevada's Las Vegas campus.

I asked, "Why? I'm happy at Columbia. I like my classes and my new friends."

Dad said, "We'll just go and look, see what the school has to offer."

I really didn't want to go, but I went along anyway, to appease my parents. As always, I allowed them full control of my life. We landed in Las Vegas on a beautiful spring day. We took a cab to the hotel, dropped off our bags, and took another cab to the university.

The campus was brimming with beautiful, green grass and exotic palm trees. A counselor was on hand to give us a tour of the school. As we walked, I was awed by the spectacle of it all. UNLV students all seemed so beautiful to me. As much as I loved Columbia and my unusual new friends there, this was somehow even better. This school appealed to the 'old,' traditional me, the one who attended a private, Catholic high school. Everyone at UNLV seemed like the students with whom I went to high school.

Everyone looked the same: preppy, refined, clean. In other words, ordinary, normal. The girls were stunning and mostly wore shorts with bathing suit tops. The guys were all handsome and in good shape, wearing shorts and tank tops.

I was enchanted by everything: the weather, the students, and all the attention I was getting. Of course, my mom wanted nothing to do with this place. She wanted me to stay home, close to her. If it were up to my mom, we would never have gotten out of the cab in front of the UNLV campus. Dad, on the other hand, liked the kind of student he saw at the university.

After viewing the campus and grounds, the counselor asked me what I thought of the university. I told her I was deeply impressed with both the school and its student body.

My mom interrupted and said, "Listen, this is a very nice school, but we will need to think about this. Can we have your card?"

The counselor said, "Of course."

As Mom hustled my father and me out, she looked at the counselor and said, "We'll be in touch."

We took a cab to the hotel. When we were back in our room, my dad said to my mom, "You didn't like UNLV, did you?"

Mom said, "I'm not sure this school can offer Patrick the education he needs. The counselor was too pushy."

Dad looked at Mom and said, "You just don't want your baby to be 2,000 miles away from you, because then you can't control his life. I want our son to grow up and be a man. Being away from home will be a good experience for him."

I had never seen Dad confront Mom like that before. This made Mom angry. She said, "We're not going to discuss this now. Let's take the brochures and talk about it when we get back to Chicago." Of course, we never had that conversation. Then one day, when I was alone with Dad, he asked me what I thought about UNLV.

I told him, "I'd love to go to school there, Dad. I know it would be good for me to get away from Chicago and the family. It would give me a chance to grow up and find myself."

Dad told me he would back me up with Mom if this is what I really wanted. So, that night at dinner I said, "Mom, I want to go to UNLV."

Mom peered across the table and said, "No, you can't. It's too far away."

Marco chimed in and said, "I think it's a great idea. Brother,

I'll come visit you all the time."

Dad said, "Look, it's no more than we're paying for Columbia."

I looked at Mom and said, "Please, Mom, I really want this."

Mom said, "If you leave, you'll never come back."

I said, "Mom, it's just college. I'll come back. I promise."

Mom started to cry and said, "If this is what you want, then go ahead."

I decided to leave Columbia for UNLV after my freshman year. My family threw me a going-away party and invited our family and all my friends. I was sad to leave, but I believed I was doing my mother and myself a big favor. I was always her baby, her favorite. Now, I was going away to college, something my sisters and brothers would never have dreamed of doing.

On the plane to Las Vegas the stewardess asked me if I was heading to Vegas for vacation.

I said, "No, I'm going to attend UNLV."

A few minutes later she came back and said, "I just met a young man up front who is also on his way to attend UNLV. I told him about you and he asked if he could introduce himself."

I thought it was a little strange but, at the same time, I felt I was on an adventure and wanted to meet new people, and maybe I just didn't understand how people outside of my neighborhood acted. I told the stewardess, "Sure, I'd like to meet him."

The guy came back with the stewardess and she introduced us.

He said, "My name is Jacob. I'm from Indiana, how about you?"

I told him I was from Chicago, and then the stewardess said to the woman sitting next to me, "These two boys are on their way to the same university in Las Vegas. They just met, and I have a feeling they're going to be good friends. Would you mind exchanging seats with this gentleman? I'll buy you a drink."

I thought it was nice to meet someone I would know at UNLV. Jacob sat next to me and we talked all the way to Las Vegas. I was instantly attracted to him. He told me about Eva, his high school sweetheart, and then he told me about his family. Jacob told me he had a beautiful younger sister, and I didn't doubt him because he was so handsome himself. Then, I told Jacob about my big, Italian-Irish family. We laughed and enjoyed talking about each other's lives.

When we landed, I called my mom as she had made me promise before I left. I told her everything was fine. I told her about Jacob, my new friend. I could tell Mom was worried about me. She said, "Patrick, please be careful when you meet new people. Don't trust anyone."

I said, "Mom, I'll be fine. Please don't worry about me."

When Jacob and I checked in on campus, we were assigned to the same dorm but to different rooms. Jacob suggested we try to get the same room. I agreed and we were able to arrange it, and so Jacob and I became roommates.

The next year at UNLV was one of the best years of my life. Jacob and I were recruited to join a fraternity and we accepted. Over time, I became friends with people from all over the world. Of course, Mom called all the time to check up on her baby.

My family came to visit me throughout the year. First, Marco and our friends came to visit. Marco had never been more proud of me. Then Mom and Dad came the week after his visit. They took me and a few of my friends to dinner at the best Italian restaurant in town. Dad was happy and proud of me because I was finally making it on my own. Mom, on the other hand, was not happy. She didn't like me living so far away from home. Upon leaving, my mom cried so hard I could feel her pain.

During my time at UNLV, Jacob and I did everything together. We had dinner together every night and partied a lot. But, there was something I could not quite understand about Jacob. We had beautiful girls at our school and they flirted with him all the time. I remember one night we threw a party in our room. Every one that lived on our floor was there including this gorgeous girl named Diane. Diane was a Tennessee beauty queen who was always flirting with Jacob and made no secret of her crush on him.

That night we all got drunk and, later, Diane passed out on Jacob's bed. My bed was right across from Jacob's so I would know if anything was going on. But, that night Jacob just slept and never made any advances on Diane. The next morning when Diane left I asked Jacob why he didn't make a move on her. Jacob replied, "I have a girlfriend back home that I love." I respected that but Diane was so beautiful and willing. Jacob's behavior puzzled me because it didn't match what I knew about how men were 'supposed' to act.

During our second semester Jacob's girlfriend, Eva, came to visit. Jacob rented a hotel room so they could be alone. During Eva's visit we all went out to bars together and had a good time. I liked Eva, but I noticed that the two of them didn't seem very affectionate, at least in public.

I started to grow more and more attracted to Jacob even

though he had a girlfriend and was demonstrably straight. At this point I had dismissed every gay impulse I had without acting on any of them. It was stupid for me *not* to explore these impulses because I was thousands of miles away from home and could do pretty much whatever I wanted to do. At times, I had urges to find a gay bar and just see what that world was like. But as soon as I gave it a thought, guilt overwhelmed me and crushed any impulses or desires I had held.

When I finished my sophomore year at UNLV, I knew I had to come home. Mom and Dad were spending their life savings to send me to school. I felt guilty. Dad was very upset at the notion of my coming home, though. He wanted me to stay in Las Vegas, but I just couldn't. I agonized over leaving UNLV because of Jacob and all of the great friends I had made. These people changed my life, and I grew up during those years.

My relationship with Jacob, although never physical, held a very deep connection and I felt we were so much more than just 'buddies.' But I never made a move on him or told him how I felt for fear of outing myself and possibly being rejected. I also did not want to risk our close friendship. If nothing else, I had a good friend that meant the world to me. I left Las Vegas in June of 1985, though I knew one day I would be back.

When I returned to Chicago it felt strange to be back; it was as if I had been gone for a lifetime. I felt like I had grown up. A part of me, though, felt like I had given up the freedom I had enjoyed living so far away from my family. Being back gave my family control of my life again, and I could no longer be myself. Being back also reminded me of the friends I had left behind in Las Vegas -- Jacob and my entire group of new friends. I also thought that I had lost the opportunity to explore living as an openly gay man. I was disappointed in myself because that may've been my only chance of coming out of the closet.

When I got home, I found out my brother Marco had purchased a motorcycle. Our mom was so angry she wouldn't speak to him. Mom hated motorcycles because some guy she dated in high school was killed on one when they were teenagers. But, I loved motorcycles and always wanted to ride one. I asked Marco if he would teach me.

Marco said, "No way, Mom will kill me if she finds out."

I begged him and he finally gave in. We would go to the school yard and practice every afternoon. I felt like he was my friend for the first time in my life, and I loved it. It took me about a week to learn to ride. Then one afternoon when Marco had to go to work, I asked if I could ride the bike alone.

Marco said, "Yeah, but I want you to call me before you leave and as soon as you get back." After that day, he let me ride his bike regularly.

One summer day, I was riding Marco's motorcycle, feeling cool. I had on tight jeans, riding boots, and a tank top. As I was riding, an attractive girl in a car passed me, beeped, and waved. I felt like a hot movie star with a beautiful young woman flirting with me. The girl pulled over and waved for me to stop and talk to her. I pulled over and she got out of her car and walked towards me. She had long brown wavy hair and amazing blue eyes. She was short, but she had a gorgeous body.

"You're Patrick Dati, aren't you?" she asked.

I said, "Yes, why do you ask?"

She said, "I'm Stella. We were in the third grade together. You disappeared the next year."

I told her I had transferred to St. Ferd's after that because my parents wanted me to go to a private, Catholic school. I didn't tell her that I flunked third grade, or why.

"I had a crush on you," Stella said.

"You're joking," I said.

Stella replied, "I did and I still do, Patrick Dati. You're as cute now as you were back then."

We talked and talked, telling each other about our lives since the third grade. Finally, we exchanged phone numbers, and I told her I would call her for a date. On our first date, I took her to an Italian restaurant owned by friends of my parents. We had a good time and after I drove her back to her parent's house, we sat in the car listening to the radio and making out.

This was the life my parents wanted for me. It was the life I thought I was supposed to live. Stella and I got along great and everyone was happy for us. It was strange because at times I still thought of Jacob. I did call him and we stayed in touch, but it just wasn't the same as it had been in the past. I wanted to rid all thoughts of Jacob from my mind so I could live out my family's fantasy for me. Stella introduced her friend, Liz, to my friend, Tommy, and we double-dated that summer and all through college. I thought Stella was the girl for me. She was someone with whom I could settle down and start a family and then live out the life my family expected of me.

My mother was thrilled. Stella would come over while I was in school and hang out and cook with my mom. They would talk about what each liked best about me. My mom thought the world of Stella.

During our senior year, Liz and Tommy got engaged and asked Stella and me to be their maid of honor and best man. We were happy for them but, shortly after, Stella started bugging me to get married.

One day we were having the marriage conversation and I told her, "I do love you and I do see a future for us, but I can't commit now. We have our whole lives ahead of us. Right now, we need to concentrate on school. I want to be rich and successful."

Stella said, "I don't care about money, Patrick. I want you."

I told her I'd worked too hard to get where I was and that I needed to make something of myself before getting married. She became upset with me after that and asked me to take her home. I felt bad that I had upset her, but I knew what I wanted and I was determined to get it. I then fully realized I had created this relationship with Stella to make everyone *else* in my life happy. I wasn't sure the life she wanted could make me happy, though. I didn't want to be tied down with a wife at home raising my kids. I wanted to be with someone that shared my dreams of success and wealth. I realized I was leading Stella on and in the end she was going to get hurt.

I was also still thinking about Jacob and what our future might have been had I stayed in Las Vegas. I was very confused and, again, I didn't feel true to who I needed to be.

I didn't call Stella for a few days after that. I needed time alone to think about the two of us and our possible future together. I realized that even though I loved Stella, I wasn't *in* love with her. I had a dream of being with someone who wanted to be rich, living a life of luxury on Lake Shore Drive. I didn't want a house like my parents, in a neighborhood like the one where they lived. I wanted to live a life my folks would be proud of, but I didn't want to live a lie. What about me, I thought. Did I have any say in what direction my life was heading?

Stella was a wonderful girl and deserved to be with someone who could give her the life she wanted. Since I hadn't called her for a few days, she came over to see me. It was a hot summer day and I was in the garage, working out. My mother was sitting in the kitchen visiting with her sister, my Aunt Holly. All the windows were open. Stella stormed into the garage and asked me why I hadn't called her.

I said, "Stella, I feel we both need time alone to think about our relationship."

She asked, "What about us? Do you love me or not?"

I said, "I do love you." But I shook my head and turned away. "You deserve better than me."

"Patrick, will you ever let anyone love you?" she asked.

I said, "I love you, but I can't say I'm *in* love with you. We want different things in life, and I don't want to hurt you."

Stella slapped me across the face and started to cry. She told me, "You will never be happy. You pull back, and you don't let people in." She ran to her car and sped away.

I was crying, and when I walked into the kitchen, my mom, who had heard everything, asked, "What are you doing with your life, Patrick?"

I replied, "Mom, can we *not* have this conversation now?"

Mom looked at me and said, "Really, what are you doing with your life? You just let the perfect woman walk away. What are you doing, my son?"

I looked at her and said, "What looks perfect to you is not perfect to me, Mom." At that moment, I wanted to tell her that I was gay and needed to live my life openly, but I figured that would have killed her.

She asked me, "What are you saying, Patrick? Stella can't be a good wife? She can't give you children? *What?*"

I said, "Mom, Stella can provide all those things, but I don't want them right now."

"When will you be ready? Don't you have dreams?" she asked.

I responded, "Yes Mom, I have dreams but they're not the same as Stella's dreams."

I grabbed my keys and left, crushed, because I had disappointed my mother and my family. Just then, I felt the need to call Jacob and tell him what I felt for him. I wanted to just 'fess up' and live my life as an openly gay man. Were it all so easy.

I graduated from college on June 12, 1987, five days after I broke up with Stella. My parents came to my graduation and were proud and happy to see one of their sons graduate from college. Even so, I could feel my mother's disappointment. She wanted Stella to be there, sitting next to her, planning our wedding at the graduation party.

Chapter 4 (1988 – 1992)
Wendy (Jacob's Sister)

After my failed relationship with Stella, I really wasn't interested in finding a life partner, though my family had different plans for me. All my siblings got married young and made Mom and Dad grandparents. I wasn't dating anyone seriously, and it drove my mother nuts. Mom later told me she had received a letter from Stella saying she was getting married. Mom kept asking me why I let her "get away."

In 1988, I started my career at a private marketing agency. It was not my dream job, but it was a job in my field. I was happy just to be working and finally making my own money. Although still living at home, I was also saving up to start a life of my own.

I was still in touch with Jacob. We talked on the phone at least once a week. I felt that this was the closest I was going to get fantasizing about what could have been. Jacob moved back to Las Vegas with his high school sweetheart, Eva, and started his career in the hotel industry. When Jacob invited me to visit the two of them, I jumped at the chance. I really wanted to get away from home and felt the need to see Jacob again, as well.

The first visit was hard because Jacob and Eva invited me to stay in their home. It gave me an opportunity to observe their relationship. I could tell Eva adored Jacob, but I still couldn't see the spark between them. On my second visit, Jacob's younger sister, Wendy, was in town. Wendy and I were introduced one night and the two of us became fast friends.

One night we were alone at dinner waiting for Jacob to get off work and join us for drinks. At one point, Wendy and I looked into each other's eyes and I felt deeply moved. She was very much like Jacob, which instantly attracted me to her. But, I was also attracted to her drive and desire to make a successful life for herself. We each had ambitious dreams for the future. Later that night, we kissed for the first time. The next day, I headed back to my family and job in Chicago.

Wendy and I started exchanging phone calls a few times a week. She told me she was going to move to Las Vegas to help Jacob with a business he wanted to start. The more I understood her drive for success, and the more she reminded me of her brother, the more my attraction to her grew. Wendy moved to Las Vegas in May of 1989, just before Jacob married Eva. Jacob had asked me to stand up for him at the wedding with Wendy.

The day of the wedding was surreal for me. I struggled to accept that Jacob was going to marry a woman, and that any chance of us being together would now be over. I somehow managed to wipe this thought from my mind and chose instead to focus on enjoying the moment with Wendy. The more I learned about her, the more I liked her. She had been homecoming queen and head cheerleader in her high school, and head of her sorority in college. Even though she was from a small town, she had accomplished a lot more than any of the other girls I had dated.

Wendy and I spent the rest of that weekend together. I convinced myself I had met my soul mate and the love of my life. In the back of my mind, though, I knew I was gay and attracted to men. But being with Wendy felt 'right' because I could be with a successful, attractive woman, make my family happy and, most importantly, appear normal.

When I got back home from the wedding, Wendy and I started talking every day on the phone. I sent her flowers every week. Romance was blooming and I thought I was falling in love. For some reason, I didn't tell my family about Wendy, and she didn't tell her family about me. I didn't want to put my mother through what she went through with Stella all over again. Wendy didn't say anything out of respect for my friendship with Jacob, her brother. We decided we would reveal our secret when the time was right for both of us.

That summer my parents, aunts, uncles, and I all went on

vacation to Las Vegas. One night my family went to dinner with Jacob, Eva, and Wendy at an Italian restaurant. Wendy sat next to me at dinner and we laughed and flirted all throughout dinner. Jacob didn't catch on, but Eva did. Eva knew about Stella, and she adored Wendy. I could see she was happy for us.

My aunt whispered to my mother that she thought there was something between Wendy and me, but Mom laughed it off because Wendy was not "my type." In my mother's eyes, *my* type was a perfect Italian girl like Stella, and by no means was she a girl with dreams and ambition like Wendy. When we got back to Chicago, my mother told me she had a funny story to tell me.

I said, "Let's hear it."

Mom said, "Your Aunt Holly thinks you and Wendy have something going on."

I looked at Mom and said, "Have a seat."

She clutched the back of a kitchen chair and gasped, "Is everything okay?"

"Mom, everything is wonderful," I said.

She said, "So, what is it?"

I said, "I think I'm in love with Wendy."

Mom looked at me and said, "You're nuts! She's your college roommate's sister. She's not even from Chicago!"

I held fast. "I've found the love of my life Mom, and it's Wendy."

My mom was speechless, probably for the first time in her life.

The next week, I told Wendy I was in love with her. Wendy said she was in love with me too, and asked, "What were we going to do about it?"

I replied, "I'm going to move to Las Vegas."

She asked, "But what about your job?"

I told her I had already spoken to my boss and asked for a leave of absence, and he approved it.

I asked Wendy not to tell anyone yet, especially Jacob. I said, "I have not told my family yet and want everyone to be surprised." 'Surprised' was an understatement considering what was soon to take place.

The next Sunday, as always, my family gathered at my parents' house for breakfast. Mom was making pancakes for her grandkids, who were screaming and running around the house. Everyone was exchanging stories and having a good time. My sister Gabriella asked me what was new with me.

I then looked around the room and asked in a full voice, "Can I have everyone's attention?" The adults all stopped talking, but the kids continued playing and laughing.

"I have something important to tell everyone," I announced.

Mom dropped the frying pan on the counter and turned to me. My sisters just stared at me. Marco stopped in the middle of a joke he was telling my brother-in-law, gawked at me, and said, "What do you have to tell us, little bro?"

I said, "I'm in love with Wendy, Jacob's sister, and I am moving to Las Vegas to be with her."

My mother turned white as a ghost. She then turned off the stove and exited the room. My sisters both got up and grabbed and hugged me. They had heard me talk about Wendy, but they didn't know we had fallen in love.

Marco and my brother-in-law both high-fived me. Dad was beside himself with happiness. I knew he approved. Then my little niece, Joann, came into the room and said to Gabriella, "Mommy, Grandma is in the bathroom crying."

Gabriella turned to me and said, "Don't worry about Mom, I'll talk with her."

My sister Maria added, "Let's get some champagne and toast Patrick."

A few minutes later, Gabriella and Mom came out of the bathroom and joined us. Mom didn't look at me; she just went back to making pancakes. A few minutes later she said, "Make room at the table, I have hungry grandchildren to feed."

Later, Mom was cleaning up after everyone had left that afternoon. I went over to her and put my arms around her saying, "Mom, don't be upset. I want you to be happy for me."

She sighed, "I want to be happy for you, but I can't stand the thought of you moving away from me."

I told her, "It will be fine. You'll see."

I moved to Las Vegas in the summer of 1990. I brought only a single suitcase of clothes with me. I left my job, my car, and my family behind. Nothing seemed to matter to me because I knew Wendy was the woman for me. I was doing what I thought a straight guy was supposed to do. Wendy picked me up at the airport and we went back to her apartment and unpacked my bags. She said, "Before we do anything else today, we need to go tell my brother the news."

I asked her, "Are you ready to do this?" Deep down inside I wasn't sure I wanted to tell Jacob I was in love with his sister, after carrying these feelings for him for years.

She told me, "Yes, I love you."

We drove over to Jacob and Eva's house and when Wendy opened the door she asked me to wait. Wendy went into the family room and asked Jacob and Eva to come and see who she had at the front door. I heard Jacob say, "This better be good."

When Jacob turned the corner and saw me he said, "Hey bud, what are you doing here?"

Wendy said, "Jacob, Patrick and I are together."

Jacob appeared shocked. He asked, "Together in what way?" I could tell from the expression on his face that he was very confused.

Eva said, "Jacob, they're in love."

Jacob stood still for a moment, and then he grabbed Wendy and hugged her. Then he walked over to me, put his arms around me, hugged me, and whispered in my ear, "You better take good care of my little sister."

We all gathered in the kitchen and poured drinks to celebrate. I was suddenly convinced that I was doing the right thing. Everything between Wendy and me was great. She was gentle, kind and loving, and she was beautiful. When she walked into a room, everyone stopped and looked at her.

I found a job as a marketing manager with a security company. Wendy and I were happy and we both had dreams of helping Jacob with his business. We met new friends and enjoyed our lives together. Mom called me every Sunday afternoon to make sure I went to church. Mom also called Jacob's wife, Eva, from time to time. Eva was from a close-knit Italian family, so Mom knew she could get the truth from her. Mom always had control of my life, even when I lived thousands of miles away.

At the end of summer, without telling anyone, I bought an engagement ring for Wendy. I drove over to Jacob and Eva's house after I picked up the ring. I wanted to ask Jacob's permission to marry Wendy. When I told Jacob and Eva, they obviously expected it, and they were pleased. In the back of my mind I hoped Jacob might object and ask me to be with him instead, but of course that didn't happen.

Jacob got us reservations at the most exclusive restaurant in Las Vegas at the time. I told Wendy that we were meeting Jacob and Eva for dinner. Of course, it would just be the two of us. I planned to have a waiter serve her a dozen roses with the ring placed on a gold platter. When the waiter approached the table, I bent down on one knee and asked Wendy to marry me. She started to cry and said, "Yes, of course."

The restaurant staff came over and started clapping. After dinner we rushed over to Jacob and Eva's to show them the ring. Wendy called her parents and they were delighted. Then it was my turn. Wendy handed me the phone and said, "Now, let's call your family."

By this time, it was late and I knew Mom and Dad would already be in bed. The phone rang a few times and then Mom picked up. I could tell she had been sleeping. I said, "Mom, it's me."

She said, "Honey, is everything okay? It's so late. What's wrong?"

I said, "Everything is great, Mom. I just called to tell you Wendy and I got engaged tonight."

The phone went silent.

I said, "Mom, are you still there?"

She said, "I'm here. That's great news honey, but it's very late. The entire family will be here early for breakfast, and I need to get up for church in the morning. Give Wendy a kiss for me and tell her I'm happy. Call back tomorrow. Goodnight, my darling."

I was not sure how to take that conversation with her. This was not the girl Mom had in mind for me, and I could tell she was not happy. The next day we called and my entire family was at my parents' house. I could hear the kids screaming over the phone, "We miss you, Uncle Pat. We love you!"

Both of my sisters talked to Wendy on the phone. They told her how thrilled and happy they were for her. Then, it was Mom's turn. She got on the phone with Wendy and said, "Dear, we love you and we're happy to have you as part of our family." She couldn't say 'I,' only 'we.' She clearly did not want me to be with Wendy, let alone marry her.

Wendy began making wedding plans with her mother. It was an exciting time for me too, but the thought of disappointing my mother was bothering me. I felt strange about being in Las Vegas instead of being in Chicago with my family.

That fall Wendy and I took a weekend trip back to Chicago to visit my family over Thanksgiving. On Thanksgiving morning, several family members headed to the park for a family game of tag football. Marco had started drinking early that day and was already drunk. When we got to the park, the game began. I was playing on Marco's team. Marco was quarterback and told me to go out for a high pass, which I missed.

He jeered, "Patrick, you sissy loser, you're such a faggot!"

Marco pushed me and said, "Come on you big sissy." Marco punched me in the face and I fell backwards onto the cement sidewalk. My lip and head were bleeding.

"Get up!" "The others were urging me saying "Hit him back!" But I just couldn't. My brother in-law looked at me and announced that I needed stitches. Once Wendy and I were done in the Emergency Room I said, "Let's go back to my parents' house."

Wendy said, "Are you crazy? Your brother beat you up and sent you to the Emergency Room! Marco is a drug addict and a drunk and I will not stand by and see him treat you like this. No, we are not going back."

I had been so excited to introduce Wendy to my family and my city, but after that incident, she was no longer impressed. When we went back to Vegas, I missed Chicago even more. I missed my family, my friends, and, strangely, my life. I loved Wendy, so I tried my best to stick it out. One day I finally told her I needed either to be in New York or Chicago to be successful in my career.

Wendy said, "But you moved here so we could share our dreams."

"I thought I could have a career in Las Vegas, but it isn't working, honey," I said.

She asked, "Do you still love me, Patrick?"

"Yes, of course. I want to marry you and spend the rest of my life with you. But we need to live in a big city where there are more opportunities for us."

Wendy sighed, "I guess this is your way of telling me we're moving to Chicago."

I promised her, "You'll love Chicago, and you'll have a better career there."

"Well, it is closer to Indiana," she admitted, "And I can see my parents more." She eventually agreed to move to Chicago in September, prior to our wedding the following May.

In truth, I was driven by the guilt of hurting my mother's feelings and my constant need to please my family. I did not know how to please myself or just be my own person. At this point I already felt I was living a lie, pleasing everyone but myself.

When I called my mother and gave her the news, she dropped the phone. I heard a huge scream on the other side of the phone, and I heard Mom crying and saying, "Butch, come here!"

Dad picked up the phone and said, "Your mother is crying. Is everything okay there?"

I told him, "Yes, Dad. Wendy and I have decided to move back."

He asked, "Is this what *you* want, son?"

I assured him it was, digging my lie in deeper and giving into my mother's persistent need for control.

Mom grabbed the phone out of Dad's hand and said, "Honey, when will you be home? I'll make everything perfect for you." Either accidentally or on purpose, Mom forgot that Wendy was joining me.

I replied, "Mom, we're coming home to find jobs and get married, not to move in with you."

Mom said, "You just made me the happiest mother in the world!" I made her the happiest mother in the world because I was doing what she wanted me to do.

Of course, when we got to Chicago, Wendy and I lived with my folks until we found jobs. When we found an apartment, it was only a block from my parents' home.

Wendy and I got married on May 23, 1992, and the wedding was everything I dreamed it would be. Jacob was my groomsman, but he came to the wedding without Eva. He told me that he and Eva were taking a break, but he was sure things would work out eventually. I thought that was strange because they both seemed to love each other so much. I tried not to focus on Jacob's obviously failing marriage. Our family and friends enjoyed the wedding, and Wendy and I were in love. It was a dream come true, even though it was my mother's dream, not mine. Everyone was so happy that I finally seemed content with my life. Yet, while people at our wedding told us we were the perfect couple, I still couldn't get my mind off of Jacob.

Chapter 5 (1992 – 1995)
Life in Suburbia

We settled into our new apartment and Wendy decorated it with her country flare. Although it wasn't my style, I didn't care. I was back in Chicago and with my family. Having that, I wanted Wendy to be happy too, and I believed that if she felt at home and comfortable in our own apartment, she'd be happy.

Wendy was a trooper. She participated in all of my family events, including the family's sacred ritual -- Sunday morning breakfast after church. I had twelve nieces and nephews and one of them was always having a birthday or recital. Wendy went to all of them with me. People make sacrifices for one another, and Wendy made a lot of them for me. Even though I love my family, I know they are sometimes a bit too much for some people.

Wendy got a job with a large insurance firm in the suburbs and concentrated on being successful. I was happy for her because she made new friends and gained some distance from my family. I got a job with a publishing company in the city and enjoyed meeting new people from the office. Wendy's parents lived in Indiana so we'd travel to see them often, which made her happy.

We were both working and making decent salaries, so we started traveling. We took trips to places like Mexico and just enjoyed ourselves. We didn't have the worries that other couples our age did. Most of my friends already had a couple of kids and were struggling financially. Of course, every time we were with family or friends, everyone would ask us when we were going to have a baby. Wendy and I wanted children, but we wanted to focus on our careers first.

After we celebrated our first anniversary, Wendy wanted to buy a home in a new community being developed in the far north suburbs.

She asked me, "Honey, can we just go look at it?"

I agreed, but I didn't want to leave the city or move away from my family. I felt most secure when I was near them. The drive to the suburbs was excruciating at nearly two hours. I was dead set against this kind of move. There were a few model homes, each postcard perfect with two stories, white picket fences, and an attached garage. While we were looking through the model homes, I noticed that the other couples looked just like us— everyone was young, professional, white, and similarly dressed. I wondered just who I had become. It felt like Wendy had transformed my appearance to model what she thought was 'perfect.'

I was so surprised, I stopped and looked in the mirror in a master bedroom and asked myself, "Is *this* who I am?" I was shocked by the realization that I was starting to live a fantasy meant for someone else. Although the people in these communities were all friendly, I realized I just wasn't one of them. I had lost the identity that I thought I once had. Wendy had built her perfect husband, and I went along with it to please her. What about me, I thought. Had I given up all control of my life?

The real estate agent gave us brochures and his business card, and told us to call him with any questions.

When we got into the car Wendy asked, "What do you think? I love it."

I said, "You have to be kidding me, Wendy."

She said, "What do you mean?"

I told her, "Look Wendy, I don't fit in that community. It's just not me."

She asked, "Why? Why do you feel that way?"

I said, "Wendy, I'm a city guy. The damn trip here took longer than it took my family to drive to Wisconsin on vacation."

Wendy looked at me and said, "Patrick, you are different from your family."

I said, "Different in what way?"

She said, "I love your family, but you all really lean on one another. No one ventures out of that world. I want to be honest with you, Patrick. Your mother controls everyone's lives."

I said, "Wendy, you are talking about the family I love, the family and world that's home to me."

Wendy said, "Don't you want your kids to have a different world? A place they can play in that's safe? I don't want to worry about someone hurting our children."

It all came back to me, then -- an innocent 9-year-old boy, trapped and raped in the men's room of a Goldblatt's department store. I stopped the car and looked at Wendy. She could see the terrible fear in my face. I said, "Maybe you're right. Can we go home and think about it?"

Wendy said, "I love you, Patrick."

A few weeks later we signed the contract to have our new home built in Round Lake Beach. Wendy was so excited she was ready to explode with happiness. When I told my mom, she said, "Are you crazy? You might as well live in Las Vegas."

One Sunday, we took my parents to see the model homes and the land on which the home was going to be built. My mom's reaction was the same as mine when we first drove out to the suburbs.

At one point she said, "Are we ever going to get to this place?"

After we showed my parents the model home, Mom said, "These homes are all hoity-toity. You don't need a home with all this fancy crap, Patrick. You need a home with character."

I said, "Mom, please be quieter, there are other people looking at these homes."

Mom said, "Where will you buy groceries? There are no stores."

When we were outside looking at the lot my father confided, "I love it."

Wendy gave him a big hug. Dad said, "I think it's great. It's a nice place away from the madness of the city."

My mother said, "No one asked for your opinion, Butch."

Dad said, "I'm happy for the kids, and I think they're making the right decision."

I didn't agree with Dad, but his words made Wendy happy and, as always, I made myself content with her happiness.

We moved into our new home in June of 1994. Everything was brand new. Even though the trip there felt endless, the home was beautiful nonetheless. Wendy's parents came in the week after we moved in and helped us get everything in shape. Her dad put screen doors on, and her mom helped Wendy decorate. I felt that I achieved another of my parents' dreams for me, but I wasn't sure anyone was pleased except Wendy. I was okay with that, actually. Our neighbors, Julia and Rob, came over to introduce themselves. I thought I was in Stepford. Everyone and everything seemed picture-perfect.

From then on, we spent our weekends with our neighbors. One weekend, they hosted the party and the next weekend, we hosted the party. I was bored and stuck on Wisteria lane, although Wendy was happy. She loved her home, her job, and me.

In March of 1995, Wendy and I went to Hawaii with my older brother, Michael, and his wife, Mary. We had planned the trip for a year and were looking forward to it. We landed on the big island and stayed at a fantastic resort. The first night there, Wendy and I made love everywhere in the room, including the balcony. We were love birds in paradise. At sunset we would walk along the ocean, and during the day, we'd lay in hammocks near the pool. One afternoon, Wendy and Mary went shopping and my brother went to Pearl Harbor. I hung out by the pool and did nothing.

I fell asleep for a while and when I woke up I noticed a young man across the pool. He looked about 22 years old, with barbed wire tattooed around his very muscular arms. His hair had blonde highlights that contrasted against his tan body. He was wearing a tight blue swim suit that hid nothing. I felt weird staring at him so I put my sunglasses on, sipped my beer, and tried to concentrate on the newspaper. Whenever I looked up, the young man was staring at me. I felt uncomfortable. I walked over to the bar and got another beer. When I sat down and looked at the man again, he tilted his sunglasses down and stared at me. I looked away nervously.

A few minutes later, I got up and went to the bathroom. When I got back, the guy had switched seats and was seated closer to me. I picked up the paper and began to read. Then I noticed the guy dive into the pool. I tried to suppress the attraction I felt towards this man. "I am not gay," I told myself. "I am married to a beautiful, successful woman."

I forced myself to not look at him. As I read, I saw his feet pass in front of my chair. Then, I heard him sit back in his pool chair, so I glanced up and realized he was staring back at me. He lifted his glasses and winked at me. Then he asked, "How is your vacation?"

I was stunned. I didn't consider myself attractive, but this guy obviously did.

He asked me, "Do you speak English?"

I looked at him and said, "Excuse me?"

He said, "Good, you speak English. Can I buy you a drink?"

I told him, "No, thank you. I have a beer."

After a brief pause, he said, "You're very handsome."

I was so surprised, I spit out my beer. "What did you just say to me?"

He said, "I think you are handsome."

I gawked at him and said, "I'm a married man."

He looked back at me and said, "That's why I said what I did."

I got up and grabbed my things and started to walk to the hotel. As I approached the entrance, Wendy came out and asked, "Where are you going?"

I said, "I got tired of waiting for you and was going back to the room."

Wendy said, "Let's go back to the pool and have a drink." We walked back and when Wendy was approaching the man I said, "Honey, let's go on the other side. There's too much sun here."

We walked away, but the man kept staring at me. That was the first time I recall a man ever hitting on me.

A few weeks after we returned from Hawaii, Wendy came home from work late. When she came in I asked where she'd been.

Wendy said, "I went to see my doctor."

I asked her if everything was alright.

She said, "I have some amazing news for you."

I said, "What?"

Wendy said, "I'm pregnant."

I was still for a second and then shouted, "Thank You, God!"

I grabbed Wendy, pulled her into my arms and held tight. I started to cry and told her, "You've just made me the happiest man in the world."

Chapter 6 (1995 – 1997)
Cynthia

The first trimester of Wendy's pregnancy was very hard on her physically as she dealt with extreme morning sickness, but things improved with time. At an ultrasound appointment, the doctor told us both that she and the baby were doing fine, and that was all we cared about. Wendy and I walked out of the doctor's office holding hands, perfectly happy.

As the due date moved closer, we prepared and decorated the baby's nursery. My parents would drive in every Sunday to drop off prepared meals Mom had made. She didn't want Wendy fussing at the stove and wanted to make sure the two of us were eating properly. In the last two months of her pregnancy, Wendy became very uncomfortable. I was told this was normal. But, she also became highly irritable. I called my sister Gabriella about this and she assured me that was normal, as well.

Wendy started spending every evening up in our bedroom, and always asked to be left alone. I was trying my hardest to make her happy, taking care of all the housework and cooking.

One Saturday I was cleaning our bathroom and Wendy came in. I asked her how she was feeling, and she replied, "Like a big, fat pig."

I asked if I could do anything for her. She watched me scrubbing the tub and said, "You can start with doing a better job with the grime on that wall."

I said, "I'm doing my best, Wendy."

She snarled, "Just leave it, I'll do it myself. You can't do anything right."

"Wendy, I realize you're uncomfortable, but getting upset with me is not going to make it better," I said.

That only made her angrier, and she yelled for me to get out of the room.

Episodes like that one became more and more common, and each one made me feel more isolated and depressed. I had seen my sisters go through multiple pregnancies, and I never knew their behavior to change so dramatically.

On one particular Sunday, Wendy was seven months along and irritable, as usual. While I was getting ready for church, I told her our neighbors had invited us to join them for breakfast at a diner in town.

Wendy said, "I'm not in the mood to be around people. Just go without me."

I left for church and came back a few hours later. Wendy was sitting in the living room watching television.

I suggested, "Maybe if you get outside and get some fresh air you'll feel a little better." Wendy yelled at me and demanded that I leave her alone.

I was so angry and frustrated that I got into the car and drove into Chicago. I thought a visit with my family might get Wendy off my mind. I parked across from my family's home, but I just couldn't bring myself to get out of the car. I knew they would ask questions about Wendy and the baby, and I couldn't deal with that. Instead, I drove to an area on the city's north side known as 'Boystown', a famous gay neighborhood near the lake. I was terrified but determined. The emotional disconnect of the pregnancy and Wendy's anger made me desperate for affection, for someone to make me feel good about myself again. My mind raced with crazy thoughts, but I pushed them away and just drove. Wearing all my masks had become too complicated. I was falling apart.

When I got to Boystown, I didn't have the nerve to go into a gay bar, so I went into a regular bar instead. While I was drinking, a guy came over and sat next to me and started talking to me. I wasn't really interested in him, but I was interested in gay sex. After some brief conversation, we headed back to his apartment where he proceeded to perform oral sex on me. I know that's what

I wanted, but I was also terrified of what would happen once I succumbed to my long pent-up desires. I crashed emotionally after the blowjob. I felt like dirt.

When I got home, Wendy was asleep. I spent the whole night praying, asking God for forgiveness and help.

The next day, I found myself overwhelmed with guilt and shame. I went to the church just behind the office building where I worked. I knelt down in front of the sanctuary and began to pray hard. As I prayed, I started sobbing. After a few minutes, I was startled by a hand on my shoulder. It was a little old lady who was cleaning the church.

She gently asked, "Young man, are you alright? I didn't mean to interrupt you, but when I heard you sobbing I wanted to reach out." In my state, she appeared like an angel to me.

I said, "I'm just upset." I told her my name and she invited me to follow her to the kitchen for some coffee. I followed her down the dark hallway. She was extremely petite, with a serene demeanor and a sweet voice. In the kitchen, she sat me down and poured me a cup of coffee. She sat down next to me and asked if I felt any better.

"Yes, you are so kind," I told her. "My wife is pregnant and we are having our first baby. I'm worried about our future." I could not tell this frail, old woman that I was praying in church because I felt guilty about having sex with a man, a total stranger.

She took my hand and said, "Patrick, you are doing the right thing coming to church and praying because God answers our prayers." That morning stuck with me as a deeply spiritual and comforting experience, something for which I was badly in need.

Things did not change at home between Wendy and me. I withdrew and began praying each night and carrying my rosary in my pocket each day. One night I was in bed, holding the Bible in one hand and my rosary in the other, praying. Wendy walked in and asked, "What are you doing? You've been up here for hours."

I told her, "I am praying for you, the baby and me."

The next morning, while we were getting ready for work, I picked up the Bible and kissed it, before tucking my rosary into my pocket. Wendy looked at me and asked, "Did you just kiss the Bible? Why did you do that?"

I said, "It makes me feel good, and I want God to answer my prayers."

Wendy scoffed and told me how strange she found my behavior. I realized the more my devotion to my prayers and rituals grew, the more distant Wendy and I became.

On March 14, Wendy called me at work to tell me she'd gone into labor. I was so excited that I ran out without my jacket or briefcase. I drove to Wendy's office and some of her friends helped me get her to the car. We went straight to the hospital emergency room and the doctor checked Wendy out and said, "You aren't ready yet, you need to wait a few more hours. You can wait here or at home." Wendy chose home.

When we got to the house she called her parents and told them the baby was coming. They immediately started the long drive from their home in Indiana. A few hours later, when her mom called to say they were almost there, Wendy told them her water had just broken. They arrived within minutes, and we all drove off to the hospital.

Wendy was in labor all throughout the night. Then, at 6am the next morning, the day before my birthday, the doctor held up a lively, purplish newborn and said, "Congratulations, you have a baby girl," as her screams began. I was crying with happiness. I had just witnessed a miracle. She was perfect. The doctor asked me to cut the umbilical cord. I was shaking but managed to make the cut. The nurse looked at Wendy and me and asked what we wanted to name her. We were speechless because we'd been expecting a boy and hadn't even thought of a girl's name. Wendy's mother leaned over the bed and said, "Her name should be Cynthia." Wendy and I loved it, so we named her Cynthia Marie.

When we brought Cynthia home, my family had already been to the house and decorated it with pink balloons and a cardboard stork in the front yard with a sign that read, "*Welcome our Baby Girl Cynthia Marie Dati.*" Wendy was in no mood to greet my family, but they were happy for us anyway. Cynthia was the youngest grandchild in the family, seven years younger than the last. I was so proud, I grinned for a week. Wendy's mother, Doris, stayed in Chicago for a week to help us settle the baby into the house. She was overwhelmed with happiness because this was her first grandchild.

After Doris left it was up to Wendy and me to take care of Cynthia. I took a few extra days off from work but soon needed to get back to the office. Wendy and I were elated to be parents, but we weren't exactly happy with each other. Wendy took to parenting as a business. She loved caring for Cynthia but clearly didn't want me around. When I came home from work, Wendy would hand Cynthia over to me and go off to the bedroom. I would care for Cynthia until I left for work in the morning and then Wendy would take over. We were both parenting, just not together.

When Cynthia was three months old, she was baptized in the Catholic Church in our town. Both of my sisters became her godmothers, because I could not choose between them. I asked Jacob to become her godfather. We had a beautiful Mass and afterwards we had a party to celebrate.

I was still acting out my obsessive prayer rituals, but it became much less noticeable after Cynthia's birth. I knew my rituals made Wendy uncomfortable, but they were my only relief from my inner turmoil. I went to Mass every morning before work. I had become friends with all the old ladies at the church and they all doted on Cynthia. When I started doing volunteer work at the church, Wendy grew angry. She resented any free time I didn't devote to Cynthia.

Cynthia was sleeping so much I worried she would get SIDS and stop breathing, so I started sleeping under her crib. Every few hours, I would put my hand on her back to feel her breathe. Meanwhile, Wendy and I grew further apart. We had not been together sexually since she found out she was pregnant. She expressed no interest in me sexually and I didn't care to ask.

One night after putting Cynthia to bed, I climbed into bed with Wendy. She was reading and I kissed her on the cheek before rolling over to say my prayers. An hour later I woke up to the phone ringing. It was Jacob. Surprised by his call, I asked him how things were in Las Vegas. He said everything was fine before asking to speak to Wendy. She started chatting with Jacob and, after a few minutes, I fell asleep again. About forty-five minutes later I woke up to Wendy sobbing. Concerned, I asked, "Honey, what's the matter?"

"It's horrible," she wept. "I don't want to talk about it right now."

"Is something wrong with Jacob or your parents? Please, if you can't tell me, I'll call him back myself and ask."

"Please Patrick, don't!" Wendy shouted. She took a deep breath and blurted out, "My brother just told me he is gay!" She started crying harder.

I said, "It can't be true, he was married to Eva. He loved her."

"That's why he left her," Wendy said.

I was suddenly consumed by fear that everyone would think *I* was gay because the two of us had been roommates. Everyone would wonder how I could not have known since Jacob was my best friend.

Wendy begged me not to tell anyone, especially my family. Neither of us slept that night. As I lay awake, I realized it had been obvious all along. I knew it in my heart when we were in college, but I ignored it for fear of rejection. A part of me was happy for Jacob, but I also regretted that he'd been closeted in college and we'd missed our chance to be together. I felt somehow betrayed.

A few days passed and then Wendy's mother called. We chatted briefly about the baby before she asked to talk to Wendy. Their conversation lasted nearly an hour. I gave them their privacy while I bathed Cynthia. When Wendy got off the phone, she came up to the bathroom with a big smile on her face.

"How are things with your mother?" I asked.

She said, "I have great news. My mother is taking you, Cynthia, and me to Las Vegas in two weeks. Jacob is living with his new partner, Ryan, and he wants us to welcome Ryan into the family."

"No way," I said. "We're not going. Cynthia is only six months old, and we are not bringing her on an airplane with all those germs."

"You don't want to go because Jacob is gay," she said accusingly.

"You're right," I said. "I don't want to see your brother prancing around with his new gay lover."

"Patrick, you're so judgmental! My parents have accepted that he's gay. Why can't you?"

"Please don't make me do this," I pleaded. "I'll stay home with Cynthia. You and your mother can go together."

Wendy continued to demand that we go as a family. I would have done anything to get out of it, but I finally agreed to go. When we landed Jacob was waiting at the luggage retrieval, handsome as ever and grinning from ear to ear. Wendy and Doris ran to embrace him. I carried Cynthia on one arm and a diaper bag on the other. Jacob approached to hug me, but I was not sure how to react. He patted me on the back and I smiled and asked him if he wanted to hold his niece. Jacob cooed over how big she was getting, and she seemed happy to bask in his attention.

Jacob said, "I am so happy you're all here. I can't wait for you to see our new place."

I felt strangely jealous that Jacob had lived the same lie I was living yet now acted as if everything was normal and he was free to be himself. Jacob had done what I wished I could do had I the courage.

Wendy and Doris filled the ride to the house with excited chatter over their trip. I just played with Cynthia, masking various mixed emotions. We pulled into the driveway and I saw this nice, new home that looked too ordinary to be home to a gay couple. As we were unloading our luggage, out came Ryan. He was handsome and young, maybe about twenty-three, with brown hair and a nice build. Like the house, he looked normal. I would not have thought of him as gay.

As we unpacked in the guest room Wendy asked, "What do you think?"

"They seem very happy," I admitted. I kissed Wendy on the cheek and said, "We'll make the best of it."

When we finished unpacking and put Cynthia down for a nap, Ryan invited us down for lunch by the pool. Again, I was struck by how ordinary everything seemed. Jacob and Ryan appeared to be just two guys living together as roommates. Later that evening, Doris took Cynthia to the guest room while the rest of us lounged around the pool. Jacob got out his blender and he and Wendy began to make margaritas. While they were in the kitchen, I was alone with Ryan, poolside. I felt awkward around him and worried I would say something stupid. I was also intimidated by him because he had won Jacob's heart, something I was obviously unable to do.

Ryan broke the silence. "So, Jacob tells me that you and he were college roommates."

"Yes," I replied, wondering why he'd brought it up. "We were, back in the old days. We also joined a fraternity together. He had every girl on campus chasing after him."

Ryan smiled, "Well, that's no surprise."

Then I stupidly blurted out, "Did you know that Jacob was married?"

He said, "Yes, he told me all about Eva. I heard she's a lovely woman."

I felt like an ass. Why was I bringing up the fact that Jacob was married and had women chasing him? Was I feeling homophobic, or jealous?

I said, "Listen Ryan, I'm sorry for bringing all of that up. I just don't know how to react to all of this."

"You mean to the fact that Jacob and I are lovers?" he asked.

"I don't mean to be ignorant," I said. "I've just never been around gay people before."

Ryan then said, "Patrick, just be yourself. Act normal. We invited your family here because Jacob loves all of you very much and wants us to be accepted."

It all started to make sense and I decided that if they were happy together, I could be happy for them.

The next afternoon, while Ryan and Jacob were out, Doris, Wendy, Cynthia and I were out by the pool. Doris said, "Wendy, let's go inside for a minute."

Wendy asked if I could stay outside and watch Cynthia. I said, "Sure, no problem."

After about fifteen minutes, Cynthia started crying and obviously needed her bottle. Cynthia was sitting in a baby-walker with wheels. I pushed her into the kitchen and went to the refrigerator to grab her bottle. Then out of the corner of my eye, I saw Doris and Wendy in Jacob and Ryan's bedroom, going through their personal belongings. They were laughing and making fun of the two in a sexual manner. I was shocked.

Just then, I turned around and realized Cynthia was gone. I ran to the back yard and eyed her strolling towards the pool. Before I could reach her, she fell into the pool. I screamed for Wendy and jumped into the pool. I flipped Cynthia over and she started screaming and crying. Wendy and Doris came running out.

"What's going on?" Wendy yelled.

I pulled Cynthia out of the walker seat and carried her out of the pool.

Wendy said, "Is Cynthia okay?"

I said, "Our daughter almost drowned."

She said, "Where were you?"

"I was getting her bottle from the refrigerator," I said. "Where were *you?*"

"My mother and I were in the living room talking," she said.

I said, "I don't think so, Wendy. I saw what you both were doing."

Wendy grabbed Cynthia from me and said, "You're an ass."

I said, "Would you like to tell your brother what you were doing?"

Doris said, "Patrick, we weren't doing anything wrong."

I grabbed my towel and shoes and said, "If that's what you want me to think Doris, fine. Your story is top-secret with me." I stormed out of the front door and walked away from the house.

I came back a few hours later and Ryan and Jacob were back making lunch. Jacob said, "Hi bro, where'd ya go?" I told him I needed some fresh air and wanted to see what the neighborhood looked like. I felt bad for Jacob. His privacy had been invaded by the family supposedly there to support his gay lifestyle. Wendy and Doris glared at me thinking I was going to say something. Neither of them spoke to me for the rest of the trip unless it had something to do with Cynthia. I didn't care because I saw a different side of both of them that I didn't respect.

When we got back from Las Vegas, my relationship with Wendy deteriorated quickly. Things between Doris and I changed, as well. When she called we no longer made small talk. She would just ask me to put Wendy on the phone. I kept thinking about how happy both Jacob and Ryan were, which only drove me back to my praying rituals.

Then one day, Wendy came home from work while I was in the kitchen feeding Cynthia.

"I bought something for you," she said. Wendy had not spoken to me in weeks, unless it involved Cynthia.

I said, "Do you mean you bought something for Cynthia?"

Wendy replied with a sarcastic 'no' and pulled a book from the bag she was holding. She threw the book on the table and said, "You need to read this" and then ran upstairs. I picked up the book and the title read, *How to Live with Obsessive Compulsive Disorder*. I took Cynthia out of the high chair and carried her upstairs. I walked into our bedroom and Wendy was lying on the bed with her face in her pillow.

I said, "What are you trying to tell me by giving me this book?"

Wendy said, "I was talking with my friend, Faith, from work and told her all about the strange things you do. Faith told me your behavior was similar to someone who has obsessive-compulsive disorder."

I said, "Wait a minute, you have been telling your friends at work about our problems at home?"

Wendy said, "The problems at home are not ours, Patrick, they're *yours*."

I said, "How dare you talk behind my back and tell people I have some illness. I am not sick, Wendy."

Wendy replied, "I told my mother and she thinks you have OCD, as well."

I said, "So now your family knows about an illness I know nothing about."

Wendy replied, "That's why I bought you the book, Patrick. I want you to read it and then make an appointment to see a psychiatrist."

"So now you are telling me I am nuts and need to see a shrink," I said.

She said, "If the shoe fits, wear it."

Then she said, "If you *don't* read the book and see a psychiatrist I'm going to divorce you."

I said, "Wendy, do you realize what you just said to me?"

She said, "Patrick, I mean it, either you fix your issues or I am leaving."

I said, "Wendy, what happened to the words we spoke on our wedding day?"

Wendy said, "What are you talking about?"

I said, "We both said, 'in sickness and in health, till death do us part.'"

She replied, "Patrick, I just cannot deal with your rituals – always reading the Bible and carrying around that silly rosary."

I replied, "Do you realize that when I pray, Wendy, it is for you and Cynthia?"

She told me, "I do not believe in all that crap. Get your life together or I am gone.

Cynthia was on the floor holding onto my leg and crying. I picked her up and wrapped my arms around her and rocked her. I said, "Baby girl, it's okay, Daddy has you." Cynthia started crying louder and I took her down stairs. Wendy slammed the bedroom door and I took Cynthia to the family room. I sat down on the rocking chair with her and sang her "Mockingbird." I whispered in Cynthia's ear, "*Now, hush little baby, don't you cry. Everything's gonna be alright. Daddy's gonna buy you a mockingbird.*"

Cynthia fell asleep in my arms. I had tears running down my face. I walked up the stairs slowly so she wouldn't wake up. I placed her in her crib and kissed her head. Then I lay down on the floor under her crib and fell asleep.

Chapter 7 (1995 - 1998)
Love, Marriage, Madness

I read the book Wendy gave me on obsessive-compulsive disorder. It really hit home with me in terms of the various rituals I acted out. It was thought-provoking to read about other individuals suffering with this same strange condition. Some individuals discussed in the book would wash their hands over a hundred times a day, often until their hands were raw and bleeding. There were even people who could not leave their homes for fear of catching germs that would make them sick [i.e., agoraphobia, mysophobia]. Others would engage in the same, often bizarre and repetitive rituals day in and out, for no apparent reason.

After reading the book, I made an appointment with a psychiatrist, Dr. Fredric Phillip. I was really nervous about seeing a shrink. What would we talk about? How would I describe my OCD? Would he think I'm crazy and cart me off to an institution? Well, this is what Wendy wanted me to do, and I thought it was worth it because I wanted to save our marriage. I loved her and wanted to make sure we stayed together for Cynthia's sake.

When I arrived at Dr. Phillip's office and entered the waiting room, it seemed normal enough. Chairs were lined up around the room and attractive paintings covered the walls. What seemed strange to me was that there was no receptionist to greet patients. There were doorbells next to each doctor's name working in the office. Above the doctors' names was a sign instructing clients to ring the doorbell when their appointment was to take place.

When I rang the doorbell I had no idea what to expect. I was apprehensive. After a few moments, I realized I had sweat running down the back of my neck. Shortly after, the door opened and a gentleman stood there wearing a plaid shirt with matching green tie. He had a smile on his face and extended his hand to shake mine.

"You must be Patrick," he said.

I replied, "Yes, that's correct."

"It's a pleasure to meet you, Patrick. I'm Dr. Phillip. Please follow me."

We walked down the hallway and entered a well-decorated office with dark brown carpeting and a pale-yellow sofa. Near the window overlooking Michigan Avenue stood a small desk with two cozy chairs facing each other. Between the chairs was a small table with a clock on it and a box of tissues.

Dr. Phillip said, "Please have a seat and get comfortable. Before we start your session I need to ask you a few questions."

I said, "Sure, no problem."

The doctor said he would ask me various questions to which I could answer yes or no. The questions were predictable enough at first: 'How old are you?', 'Are you married?', 'Do you have children?' Then came the more unusual questions: 'Have you ever attempted suicide?' and 'Have you ever *thought* about committing suicide? By this point my hands had become moist and clammy, and I answered the questions with some hesitation. After the doctor finished these questions he said, "Well, we have that out of the way. Now, let's talk about you."

I was not sure how to respond. I said, "Do you mean why I am here to see you?"

He said, "Sure."

I told him my wife believes I have this condition called obsessive compulsive disorder.

"Well Patrick, what do *you* think? Do you think you have this condition?"

I said, "Well, I guess."

Then he said, "Can you tell me when you thought you first had OCD?"

I said, "A few weeks ago, when my wife gave me a book about it."

He said, "So Patrick, what you are saying is before your wife confronted you about the condition, you did not know it existed?"

I told him, "I did not know about the condition, although the rituals I was acting out always did seem strange. They were coming from my brain, and I didn't understand how to control them."

"Can you describe what your rituals are and what brings them on?" the doctor asked me.

I replied, "Whenever I am nervous or something bad happens I immediately start praying and carry around my rosary and prayer book with me."

I told Dr. Phillip more about my OCD-like behaviors and what prompted them. But I didn't tell him about the rape. I just couldn't. Up until now, I had never told *anyone* about that terrible day.

When the session was done Dr. Phillip said, "I'm going to prescribe some medications that should help you control the OCD and depression, Patrick."

Dr. Philip prescribed two medications, Alprazolam, an anti-anxiety agent, and Lexapro, a newer anti-depressant at the time.

He told me, "It will take about two weeks until you start feeling an effect with the medications. I'll schedule next session for three weeks from now. Then we can see what progress you've made."

Then the doctor handed me his card. He pointed out both his home and work numbers and said, "Patrick, do not hesitate to call me if you need to talk."

I thought the session went well, and I felt good about having my OCD treated at last. Deep down I knew my need to see Dr. Philip went much deeper than just treating my OCD. I needed to deal with my feelings about the rape and, most importantly, my sexuality.

When I left the doctor's office that day, I believed he could fix all my emotional issues. I thought, overtime, he could resolve the trauma of the rape, 'cure' me of being gay, and make me straight so I could continue my family life with Cynthia and Wendy. This would solve all my problems, I figured. I could continue to hide how I really wanted to live and, instead, do what would make everyone else happy. I felt that if Dr. Phillip could mend these issues in my head, I could live happily as a straight man and bury all my conflicted and confused emotions deep inside.

I was excited to tell Wendy about my session with Dr. Phillip. It gave me new hope about our future together. I thought the doctor would cure me and we would be the perfect couple again, problem solved. When I got home that day Wendy was in the kitchen feeding Cynthia. Cynthia was sitting in her highchair with food all over her face. When she saw me, she reached out her hands and cried, "Da-da!"

Wendy said, "Damn it, this kid is so attached to you."

I said, "Well, what do you expect, I'm her father."

Wendy replied, "Well, you spoil her."

I said, "Come on Wendy, she's a baby."

Wendy said, "Well, it looks like she is not going to finish eating so just pick her up. That's obviously what she wants."

I picked Cynthia up and she stopped crying that very instant. I wiped her face with a rag and gave her a big kiss.

"So Wendy, do you want to hear how my session with the psychiatrist went?" I said.

"Sure, what did he say?"

"He did confirm that I have OCD and he put me on medication to help with the condition," I said.

"So does that mean you will not be doing any more of your stupid praying rituals?" she asked.

"Wendy, that is offensive. OCD is a condition due to lack of serotonin levels in a person's brain. With medication and support I can beat this thing. Isn't that what you want for us?" I asked.

"Patrick, do this for you and for Cynthia, not for me," Wendy said.

"What do you mean 'not for you'? I said.

"I want you to get better, but it is *not* going to save our marriage," she said.

I was stunned. I said, "You told me that to save our marriage, I needed to read the book you gave me and see a psychiatrist."

Wendy said she didn't want to have 'this conversation' right now and ran upstairs and slammed the bedroom door.

Over the next few days Wendy withdrew from me altogether. She was taking phone calls from her mom with the door closed and I could hear them whispering. Then she started making weekend plans with friends from work and asking me to stay home with Cynthia. I talked to my cousin Lisa about the situation because she loved Wendy.

Lisa told me, "Maybe you two need to go to marriage counseling. I know other people who have done it and it helped save their marriages."

I told Lisa I was willing to do anything. "I cannot live without Wendy," I said.

Lisa told me, "Patrick, it is all going to be fine because I know Wendy loves you."

The next day I looked up some marriage counselors and found one near Wendy's office.   When I went home that night I told Wendy that I loved her and wanted us to go to counseling.

She said, "I am not going to counseling.   There is nothing wrong with me."

"Wendy, that is not fair. I did what you asked of me. Can we just try it? I'm begging, please," I said.

She reluctantly agreed. "I'll give it one try, but if it doesn't work, that's it," she said.

I made the appointment and we went a few days later to meet with the counselor.

The day of our first meeting, Wendy's friend, Faith, picked her up for work so we would not have to drive two cars. When Wendy got in the car that afternoon, I could tell she didn't want to do this. As I drove to the counselor, I took Wendy's hand from her lap.

Wendy looked at me and said, "What are you doing?"

I replied, "Holding my wife's hand."

She replied, "For what purpose?"

"Wendy, I love you, and I want to hold your hand," I said.

She grabbed her hand back and said, "I am in no mood to hold your hand, Patrick."

I felt so rejected. We drove in silence the rest of the way.

When we got to the counselor's office we all sat in one room together. The counselor started by asking Wendy and me what was wrong between us.

I started off by saying, "You see, we had a baby last year. We both work full time and it has put a lot of pressure on our marriage."

Wendy glared over at me and said, "That is not why we're here today, Patrick. Tell the man the truth."

I was dumb-founded and just stared at her.

Then Wendy declared, "We are here because Patrick has some condition called OCD and doesn't know how to act normal."

Angered, I replied, "So, you're telling this man I'm a freak because I have OCD?"

"You *are* a freak!" Wendy cried.

I got up from the chair and said, "Is that what you think about the man you love?"

Wendy got up and stood with her hands on her waist and spit out these words: "Patrick, I *don't* love you anymore. And I want a divorce."

I shook my head slowly. "You don't love me anymore because I have OCD?"

The counselor said to us, "Let's calm down. I would like to do a one-on-one session with Wendy right now. Patrick, would you mind waiting outside?"

I walked out the door feeling like Wendy had just ripped my heart out. After about a half an hour, the counselor came out and said, "Patrick, you can come in now."

I looked at Wendy and knew it was over. Resigned, I replied, "There's no use continuing this conversation. It's over. We can leave now."

I stormed off to the car with Wendy following. When we got into the car and drove off, Wendy turned on the radio. I clicked the radio off.

She said, "I want to listen to the radio."

"Wendy, you just told a stranger that you're no longer in love with me and now we're supposed to listen to the radio?"

I pulled the car off the busy road and put it into park. I said, "Wendy, look into my eyes and tell me you do not love me anymore."

She looked in my eyes and said, "I do not love you anymore, Patrick." She said, "I love you as Cynthia's father, but I am not in love with you anymore."

I started to cry as she stared at me with no sign of remorse. I grabbed her hand and started to kiss it, telling her over and over that I loved her. She pulled her hand back and said, "You're pathetic" and jumped out of the car.

I tried to chase her but gave up after just a few steps. I got back into the car and drove around the block to see if I could find her. I couldn't see her anywhere. Nervous, I pulled over at a gas station and called our neighbor, Alyssa, who did daycare for Cynthia. Alyssa's husband, Richard, answered the phone. Richard and I had become good friends since Wendy and I had moved into the house.

Richard said, "Hi, Patrick."

I said, "Listen Richard, Wendy and I just got into a big fight and she is out on the street alone. I'm worried sick about her.

Richard then said, "Patrick, Wendy just called Alyssa and asked her to meet her near the airport."

I said, "Are you kidding me?"

Richard said, "No Patrick, Alyssa is on her way to meet Wendy now."

I said, "Do you know where Alyssa is meeting her?"

He said, "Sorry bud, I have no idea."

I felt like everyone saw this coming except me. How could I have not noticed that Wendy was falling out of love with me? What made me think there was still hope for us?

When I pulled into the driveway, I felt like all the neighbors had long known what was going on between Wendy and me. I mean, they all knew we were having problems, but it seemed like I was now living in a ghost town. I looked at my neighbors Alyssa and Richard's house. The lights were on, but the drapes were drawn. I pulled into the garage and went into the house to call Wendy's parents in Indiana.

Doris answered the phone and I said, "Doris, have you heard from Wendy?"

Doris answered with a quick response, "No, not a word, Patrick."

I suddenly realized what was going on. Doris had this calmness in her voice and never asked why I'd be calling to check on Wendy.

Then Doris said, "If I hear from her I will be in touch" and hung up the phone.

I was set up by the woman I loved and her mother. I started to feel paranoid. I double locked every door in the house like a caged animal. I thought about calling the police but I had nothing to report. My wife had only been gone for two hours. What would they do about it?

I ran up to our bedroom and started going through all of Wendy's dresser drawers. I found everything I was looking for in her underwear draw. There was a letter from her mother dated March 16th of that year, the date of my birthday. The letter from Doris said that they understood why Wendy fell out of love with me. The letter continued to read 'Enclosed is a check for the first payment for your divorce attorney.' Doris also wrote 'Your father and I want you to move back home so make sure your attorney knows that.'

Then I found Wendy's diary, the one she'd started after Cynthia was born. Her diary reported, 'I feel bad for Patrick, but I am just not in love with him anymore. Patrick is sick with OCD and I cannot stand him anymore. When he touches me, I want to run away.' Wendy also wrote that she wanted to be back in Indiana with Cynthia and live far away from me. I cried for hours on the bedroom floor. Then, I took my medication and some sleeping pills so I could sleep.

When I woke up the next morning, I called my boss and said that I was not feeling well and wouldn't be into the office that day. I was now able to think more clearly. *How could I have been so stupid to allow Wendy to destroy my life?*

I got dressed and pretended I was leaving for work. I knew that our neighbor Julia from across the street had been watching our house and was now suspicious of her. I drove around the block and snuck to the back of my home. I then entered through the back deck of the house. I sat in a rocking chair staring at the door that leads to the garage. Within a matter of minutes, I heard the garage door open and in through the door came Julia. When she saw me sitting in the chair she looked shocked.

I said, "Is there something I can help you with Julia? Did you come over for a cup of sugar?"

She was lost for words and began to stutter. Then she said to me, "I thought you left."

I said, "You did? What do you want here, Julia?" I demanded.

"I came to get some things for Wendy and Cynthia," she replied.

I said, "Why is that?"

She said, "Because Wendy asked me to."

I said, "If that's the case, you know where she is, right?"

Julia said, "I don't know where she is, Patrick."

I said, "Then what were you going to do with her things?"

"Wendy asked me to drop her things off at her office, and then someone would get them to her," she told me.

I said, "Listen Julia, are you going to tell me where my wife and child are?"

"Honestly Patrick, I don't know where they are," she declared.

I said, "If that is your answer, you better get out of my house right now, before I call the cops and have you arrested for trespassing."

Julia said, "Really, is that how you're going to be Patrick, we're friends."

I said, "Julia, it looks like you have two options: tell me where my wife and child are or stay here for as long as it takes me to call the police."

Julia said, "Patrick, I'm leaving. Please don't call the police."

That day the phone kept on ringing but I didn't pick up; I let the answer machine retrieve all the calls. Several of them were calls from Doris, but she didn't leave any message. My mother called several times saying she'd tried reaching me at work but was told I was home sick. Both of my sisters called because Mom told them I was not answering the phone. Truth is, I didn't want to speak to anyone. My heart was racing and I knew that if I did not grab control of the situation I would lose my mind.

I finally decided to get legal assistance while Wendy was gone and learn about my rights. I found an attorney, and we met the next day. I told him the entire story, including the fact that my wife and child were missing. A week went by and still no call from Wendy. I tried calling Doris but she wouldn't answer her phone. I knew Wendy was in Indiana and it frustrated me that she wouldn't contact me.

I called my attorney at the end of the week and he told me that if Wendy was not in town by the end of the second week, we could have her arrested for kidnapping. He asked if I knew the name of Wendy's attorney. I did, because it was on the check Doris had sent. My attorney tracked Wendy's attorney down and told her that if Wendy was not back in the state of Illinois by the following day, we would file a police report for kidnapping. These were extreme precautions, but now I was focused only on my and Cynthia's future.

Wendy and Cynthia returned home the very next day. It was tragic that our relationship had to end this way, but I felt Wendy drove me to these severe measures. At this point, though still living in the same house, we no longer were speaking to one another. We both took care of Cynthia but at different times. When I was home with Cynthia, Wendy would not come home until we were both in bed. At one point, Wendy's father contacted me at work and told me if I gave up my fight and just let Wendy move to Indiana he would pay me $10,000 in cash. I replied, "You have to be kidding me," and hung up the phone.

The saddest thing of all was that Cynthia was caught in the middle of all this bitterness. She was just a baby with parents who both loved her but could not remain together to settle matters concerning her future.

We put the house up for sale and it sold right away. I had no choice at this point but to move back in with my parents. I was paying child support and all the bills. I couldn't even afford to rent an apartment by this time.

I had Cynthia every other weekend and it was confusing for her. Before, she had me every day; now it was every other weekend. When I dropped her off on Sundays she would cry and say, "Daddy, please don't go!" It broke my heart. Maybe the worst part of all of this mess was that I still thought I was in love with Wendy. I would take her back in a heartbeat to keep our family together and give Cynthia a normal life. What did I know about a normal life? I hadn't been normal since I was a young child.

My parents would drive back with me to the suburbs every weekend to take Cynthia home. My mom watched me cry all the way back to the city.

One day she said to me, "Honey, I cannot believe how much misery that bitch has put you through. Please don't cry."

Months passed and we went on waiting for the divorce to be settled, but one of us would not agree to something the other wanted. We fought in court for months. During all this time, I still wore my wedding ring and had pictures of Wendy and Cynthia in my office.

One day, one of my friends from work, Mark, came into my office and said, "Buddy, when are you gonna take those pictures of Wendy down? And how long are you going to continue to wear that wedding ring?"

I said, "Mark, maybe she'll come back and tell me she loves me again."

Mark looked baffled and said, "Patrick, she is *not* coming back. I hate to see you put yourself through all this."

I had a department meeting at work that afternoon. When I returned to my office after the meeting, all the pictures of Wendy had been taken down and placed in a brown paper bag next to my desk. I was upset with Mark for doing this, but I realized he was just looking after me.

One weekend when I had Cynthia, my sister went with us to the grocery store. When we were in the store shopping, I saw a husband and wife holding hands while pushing their baby in the cart. I was holding Cynthia in one arm and pushing the cart with the other when suddenly I stopped and stared at them and then began to cry.

My sister looked at me and said, "Hand Cynthia over me, Patrick." I handed Cynthia to my sister, Gabriella.

Gabriella then said, "Why are you crying?"

I said, "Look how happy that couple looks." I then said, "I cannot get Wendy out of my mind, Gabriella. I love her and want her back."

Now I was crying harder.

My sister said, "Look at me, Patrick."

I looked at Gabriella and she slapped me across the face. She then said, "Get over that woman and get on with your life. You have a child to raise and you need to get over Wendy, now."

Then one day when I dropped Cynthia off at the house Wendy was renting, I noticed a truck parked in the driveway. It had been six months, and now Wendy was dating a man named 'Jim'. Jim was the brother of Wendy's friend, Faith. A few weeks later he moved in. I had lost my wife completely, and she wanted to take my child from me. My heart was broken, but truly I needed to move on.

Chapter 8 (1998 – 2002)
Life with Jennifer

Throughout 1998, my divorce from Wendy dragged on and on, with no apparent end in sight. I was becoming increasingly desperate for it to be over so I could get on with my life.

One night, I agreed to meet my friend Jack for drinks at a nightclub we'd often frequent after work. There would have been nothing memorable about that particular evening were it not for Jennifer, the person to whom Jack introduced me. Jennifer was a beautiful young woman who worked as a stockbroker with a large financial institute and had dreams of eventually running the organization someday.

After our initial introduction and polite conversation - the usual "and what do *you* do" chat - I didn't really pay much attention to her. Towards the end of the evening, Jack asked me what I thought of Jennifer.

"Not that interested, really," I replied.

So, I was surprised when Jennifer asked me out as we were leaving the bar. I was unsure how to respond, so I gave her my business card. A few days later she called me and asked if I wanted to join her for dinner. I reluctantly agreed. The truth was that I had no desire for intimacy at that point in my life. I hadn't thought of being with a man or woman in a long time. My mind was consumed with ending the divorce, my future with Cynthia, and how I was going to pick up the scattered pieces of my life.

After going out with Jennifer a few times, I found myself once again in a dating relationship, which was strange considering how little the two of us had in common. Jennifer came from a wealthy family and lived an upscale life, with a beautiful condo in River North and an expensive car.

As time passed, I began enjoying being with her because she was so different from other women I had dated, or so I thought. Looking back, I realize I had these same thoughts about Wendy, and look what happened there.

Wendy was anxious to finalize our divorce because she and Jim had gotten engaged and were planning their wedding. I was upset that Wendy was getting married. Just because you end a relationship doesn't mean you simply shut off your emotions, I figured. Getting a divorce under the law isn't the same thing as divorcing yourself emotionally from a person you loved.

Whatever the case, I needed to bounce back, and Jennifer seemed like someone who could help me do that. She knew I had a child and that Cynthia was the primary focus of my life. On the weekends I had Cynthia, Jennifer wanted no part of us. She would tell me to call her after I dropped Cynthia off with her mother on Sunday afternoons. This should sound awful to anyone with children, but it didn't bother me at all. In fact, it was a relief because, had Jennifer wanted to be included, I would have felt obligated to bring her along. This way, I had more time just for Cynthia and me.

But my relationship with Jennifer didn't feel real. It felt phony. It didn't seem like she was with me for love or companionship, and I wasn't really attracted to her sexually. The best way to describe it was as a relationship of convenience.

If Jennifer phoned me, we talked. If she didn't, I was not at all bothered. I had never felt this way in a relationship before, but what did I know about relationships anyway? I had been confused about who I was my entire life. Why try and figure things out now? I had always lived for everyone but myself, anyway.

Dating Jennifer seemed easy to me. But 'easy' is never really all that easy in the long run. I just hadn't figured that out yet.

Jennifer spent long hours at the office with her boss. One time early in our relationship, she told me she had a business trip to New York and asked if I could drop her off at the airport. She told me she would be staying at the Park Hyatt, but if I needed to reach her to call her cell phone. The fact that Jennifer would specifically tell me that made me realize she did not want me to call the hotel.

Of course, I had to call the hotel.

Just as I suspected, when I called I was told there was no one registered under her name. When I picked her up at the airport, I mentioned that I had tried to reach her there.

She told me that the hotel had been overbooked and so her boss had stayed with the client and she took his room. It was obviously bullshit. To be honest, I didn't really care. I just would have preferred she tell me the truth. I dropped her off that night and returned home.

The next day Jennifer called me at work and asked if I could have dinner with her that night. I saw it coming, and I welcomed it. She broke up with me over dinner.

"You're a great guy, Patrick, but it's just not working," she said.

Frankly, it was really no big deal to me. I was neither hurt nor depressed. I just didn't care. I told her to have a nice life and exited the restaurant having absolutely no idea of the impact this woman would eventually have on my life.

When I told my friends Jack and Mark about what happened, they were both supportive, but I could tell Mark knew more than he let on about Jennifer. I asked him if there was something he wanted to tell me, but he wouldn't tell me whatever it was. I didn't press him, though, as I was completely over the relationship as soon as it had ended, if not earlier.

In hindsight, I probably should have been a little more insistent in questioning Mark, although it may not have changed anything.

A few months later, Mark, Jack, and I decided to go to the singles party at the Art Institute in downtown Chicago. It was an elegant gathering for young professionals to meet up, and that particular night the place was packed. My life had calmed down considerably since I'd last seen Jennifer. My divorce was final, Wendy and I were starting to get along, and things were just more relaxed. I felt that it was time to start enjoying life once again.

I spent most of the night checking out good-looking guys in suits, but every once in a while I'd point out a hot woman to Jack or Mark just to keep up appearances. I was pretending to be what my friends expected of me.

Later, we were walking around the museum when we spotted Jennifer with some of her friends. Jack went over and greeted them while Mark and I hung back. I was a little uneasy and didn't really feel like approaching her, but Jennifer came right over when she saw me and was perfectly friendly, asking me how I'd been.

This all would have been fine except that, by this time, Mark had a few martinis in him and felt the need to intervene. He approached Jennifer and said loudly, "What the hell do you think you're doing?"

"We're just talking, Mark," she said, clearly taken aback by his belligerent tone.

"You fucked with my friend's heart!" he hollered, and it just got worse from there. Mark told Jennifer that he knew what she'd done to me and wanted her to stay out of my life from now on.

It all happened very quickly, but as soon as I realized Mark was on the verge of creating a major scene at an Art Institute singles night, I grabbed his arm and told him we needed to leave. Thankfully, he listened to me. I quickly said goodbye to Jennifer and left. Once I got Mark alone, I confronted him.

"You want to tell me what all that was about?" I asked. I remembered how it seemed like he'd been keeping something to himself, so I figured after that outburst he might finally be ready to tell me what was bothering him.

He was ready, and then some.

Mark ran the account for Jennifer's firm at our company, and he'd heard that Jennifer was having an affair with her boss, who was married with children. Mark hadn't told me this because he thought it would hurt my feelings. I had actually found out about the affair through the grapevine, on an earlier occasion. I never told anyone that I knew, because the *real* story would have been even more salacious. I was involved with a woman who was cheating on me with her married boss ... and I didn't care.

After a few weeks passed, Jennifer sent me an email telling me it had been nice to see me. She apparently still didn't understand Mark's behavior that night, so I told her he was just an over-protective friend and ended the communication on a polite note.

I really assumed that would've been the end of our communication, but then Jennifer sent me another email, this time suggesting we soon meet for drinks. I accepted. *But why?*

To be honest, I was asking myself that very question as I typed "Why not?" into the reply field and then hit 'send.'

We met at a swanky singles club. Things were going well at our table, the drinks were flowing, and we were having a good time.

Then, Mark showed up.

Neither of us saw him having drinks with a client at the bar, but he saw us. A few minutes later, I was standing at the urinal in the men's room when someone comes over and slaps the back of my head -- an altogether unsettling experience when you're in the middle of a piss. You don't know whether to turn around or zip up.

To my surprise, it was Mark. I gathered myself and turned around to face him.

"Why the hell are you here with that bitch?" he demanded.

"It's harmless," I told him. "She just wants to talk."

"She's nothing but trouble, buddy," Mark said.

"Mark, I'm a grown man," I replied. "I appreciate you watching out for me, but I can take care of myself."

While it's true that I was a grown man and appreciated what Mark was saying, that last part would prove debatable in the years to come, especially as it concerned Jennifer. In hindsight, I really should have listened to Mark more often.

Jennifer and I began seeing each other again, and within a few weeks, we went public with our relationship. Needless to say, this news did not go over very well with my family and friends. After watching me go through so much grief with Wendy, they were all really starting to see a pattern emerge.

Jennifer and I had been dating seriously for about three months when she asked me if I wanted to marry her. I was shocked. I mean, we were dating but, in my heart, I knew I was still a gay man. I looked at our relationship as just part of the façade that I'd built around my life, something to shelter me from a disapproving world. So, while I was *physically* with Jennifer, I was never emotionally with her. Certainly, not in my heart.

After my initial shock wore off, I told Jennifer that I would indeed marry her. She was happy, though as she hugged me and we celebrated, I could not help asking myself, '*What the hell are you doing?*' It was like I was trying to prove something to myself. Just what, I didn't truly know. Maybe I needed to prove that I could succeed in the straight world, that I could fool them all, even myself. Or maybe I thought that since it was my life, I could screw it up if I really wanted to. Which was true, of course, but who in their right mind would actually want to screw up their own life?

That last question provides its own answer.

We didn't tell anyone the big news right away. Jennifer wanted to wait until we had actually gotten engaged. She wanted a ring from Tiffany's, of course, but with my recent divorce expenses, there was no way I could afford something like that.

"That's okay," she said. "I'll buy it myself.

"Are you sure?" I asked.

"Look, I need a ring that fits my style," she assured me.

I had to agree with that. I couldn't see her happy with some shiny trinket from Macy's.

She then said, "I also make way more money than you do, so I can afford it."

No argument there, either.

"No one has to know, Patrick," she assured me. "It will be our little secret."

I thought it was all a little odd, but maybe she was right. I could never have afforded the ring she picked out.

After I picked up the ring, I took her out to dinner at one of her favorite restaurants; it was there that I proposed to her. I got up from my chair, knelt down on one knee, and asked her to marry me. She acted as if she didn't know what was going to happen. As I said the actual words, "Will you marry me?" I looked around the room and realized everyone in the restaurant was watching intently.

Just as Jennifer had wanted.

Jennifer looked around the room, took in her perfect moment, and said, "Yes," at which point I asked another question, not of her but of myself. It wasn't out loud though, but rather in my head.

What the hell are you doing?

We rushed back to Jennifer's place and she called her family, and that evening I went back to my parents' house and told my family.

My mother asked a version of the question I'd recently posed myself, namely, *"What the hell is wrong with you?"*

"Mom –"

"You don't love her!" she shouted. "Why are you getting married to a woman you don't love?"

Good question, really.

"Maybe getting married will help me get my life back on track," I explained.

My mom just shook her head. "You're my son and I love you, but you're wrong, Patrick. I love you, but you're doing the wrong thing, and you're going to get hurt again," she said.

"I'm a big boy and I can take care of myself, Mom," was all I could say, and boy was I wrong. Again.

Now that *that* was settled, the real nightmare could begin: Planning the wedding.

I had already started the annulment process for my marriage

to Wendy with the church. Jennifer gave me the cash so we could rush the process along.

Once I had the annulment, we went to Jennifer's church, Holy Name Cathedral, and set a date. The first date they had available was November 18, 2000.

Yet another day that would change my life forever.

Jennifer wanted a big spectacle of a wedding and, naturally, money was no object. We booked the top floor of the Hotel 71, a beautiful hotel in the heart of downtown Chicago. We invited 350 guests, mostly Jennifer's co-workers from her financial firm, including her boss and his wife.

On the day of the wedding, Jennifer insisted we take photographs before the ceremony. She wanted to make sure the pictures were perfect, and that meant not a single hair could be out of place. We all gathered in the large banquet room on the top floor of the hotel for several hundred pictures.

Everyone looked great, including Jennifer. She spent thousands on her wedding gown and it showed. When we were finished, it was time for everyone to leave for the church. Jennifer and her bridesmaids all left in their limo, but the guys all stayed for one last drink before hitting the road.

I should mention at this point that the one thing I insisted upon for our wedding was that Mark be one of my groomsmen, to which Jennifer vehemently objected. But I'd gone along with everything else, so she eventually acquiesced.

As we were piling into the limo, Mark pulled me aside and whispered in my ear.

"I've got two thousand bucks in my pocket right now, buddy. Let's take cab to the airport and get out of town."

"Mark –"

"Don't go through with this, Patrick," he pleaded. "You know it's wrong."

I just looked at him. "Mark, I appreciate it, I do. But there's three hundred and fifty people out there waiting to see me get married. We need to go."

"I'll support you, but in my opinion you're making the biggest mistake of your life," Mark said.

We got into the limo.

All the way to the church all I could think about were Mark's words of warning.

And, of course, he was right.

I desperately wanted to take his advice and call it all off, but it just seemed too late for that, now. All those people at the church – family, friends. How could I let them all down?

I was ashamed of myself. I knew the wedding should not be taking place. How did I let things get so out of control? What was I doing?

I began to get more and more nervous. My head was a jumble of confusion and panic. Sweat was trickling down my face.

"Patrick, you okay?" Jack asked. "You're looking a little pale."

"I'll be fine. Just give me a beer from the cooler."

Mark just shook his head, and as I took the beer, he leaned over and whispered, "Patrick, why are you doing this?"

The other groomsmen were starting to wonder what was going on. "Everything is just fine, guys. Really."

But of course, nothing was fine.

As we walked into Holy Name Cathedral, I was a mess. I was shaking like a leaf, sweating profusely and feeling downright ill.

My brother Marco, who was my best man, stepped over to me. "You okay, brother?"

"Just a little nervous, but I'll be fine," I mumbled.

As Marco and I walked toward the front of the church before the ceremony, I couldn't help but notice that every face on the groom's side held the same expression:

What the hell are you doing, Patrick?

None of my family and friends thought this was a good idea.

The other side of the church was filled with unfamiliar faces -- Jennifer's work friends, I assumed.

I wonder if they could tell how uncomfortable I was.

The priest directed my brother and me to the vestibule at the front of the church, where we were fitted with microphones. After a couple of minutes, the priest entered the room and said the words that struck terror in my heart: "Patrick, I need you on the altar now."

I looked at the priest. "Father, I need a few minutes by myself."

He nodded sympathetically. I'm sure he'd heard those words before.

"Five minutes," he said. "We have a wedding right after yours."

I guess the Father's sympathy only extended as far as scheduling would allow.

"That's fine," I said. I then told Marco to go out to the altar with the priest and I'd join them in a moment. Alone in that little room, I was finally able to breathe, but it was hardly a relaxed moment.

I don't want to marry this woman. I don't love her. I just want to live my own life!

At that moment, I actually decided to call it off. It didn't even sound crazy to me. I would just walk out to the altar and tell everyone I was sorry but that this was all a big mistake.

Immediately, I felt better. Like an enormous burden had just been lifted from my shoulders. I wasn't even worried about how everyone would react; I had made the decision I knew to be right, and that was the course I would take.

Simple, right?

I peeked out the door. The church was filled with expectant guests. The wedding party had just walked down the aisle and was about to start the wedding march. But I was still on board with my newfound courage. I was ready to stand my ground.

And then I saw my daughter.

My sweet Cynthia, my precious little flower girl, was eagerly waiting at the back of the church to walk down the aisle, followed by Jennifer and her father.

How would my daughter feel when I told everybody the wedding couldn't go forward? I imagined the very worst, with angry shouts and epithets, all directed at me, Cynthia's dad. What would she think? How would she be affected?

I decided I had to do it, anyway. Cynthia would want her daddy to be happy, right?

I took a deep breath and walked out to the altar, taking my place on the podium. Everyone looked up. I cleared my throat.

"I have something to say," I said.

You could hear a pin drop.

Everyone in that church was staring at me.

Wondering.

Worrying.

All except one person.

Straight down the aisle, Cynthia was waving at me with a big smile on her face. She wasn't wondering anything. She wasn't worried about anything. She was just waiting for her big moment, when she could walk down the aisle and make her daddy proud.

I looked at her sweet face and knew I couldn't disappoint my little girl.

"What I wanted to say was that I really appreciate all of you joining Jennifer and I for our big day," I said.

As I stepped down from the podium and took my spot, my mother caught my eye from the front row. "You ass," she whispered.

My failure to tell the truth at that crucial moment was a crushing blow for me. I was terribly disappointed because I went through with that entire farce just to please my daughter. Once again, I was living a life that pleased everyone but me.

Jennifer marched down the aisle with her father, smiling as if it were the happiest day of her life. But she wouldn't have been smiling if she knew what I was thinking. Before I knew it, it was all over, and once again I was married.

Although this was yet another life-altering event for me, I wouldn't learn its real lesson for several more years.

Shortly after our wedding, Jennifer was promoted to vice president of her Chicago office, which included a big raise. Without discussing it, Jennifer told me that she was going to buy us a new home in a wealthy, gated community. I was not interested in moving, but Jennifer always got what she wanted, including me.

The homes we looked at were very large, and priced over a million dollars.

"Jennifer, this is silly," I protested. "What do we need with all that space?"

She told me she needed to keep up with the VPs at her office, and a large home was a necessity. In other words, it was like her engagement ring. She wanted a large home for her lifestyle and that was all there was to it.

We bought a place in Park Ridge with seven bedrooms, four bathrooms, and a gorgeous chandeliered entrance with an open staircase to the second level. It was beyond anything I had ever imagined living in.

Jennifer spent thousands of dollars on new furniture to fill all of the rooms.

She also bought me a brand new BMW, and gave me credit cards to "buy some stylish new clothes" so that when I attended business functions with her, I'd look successful.

They say money can't buy happiness, but there is no shortage of people who aren't trying to prove otherwise. Jennifer was certainly one of those people. I even got caught up in her enthusiasm for a time, but before long I was just as miserable as before.

Jennifer didn't care for my weekends with Cynthia, and would usually try not to be home. When she was home, she treated both of us poorly. To her, my daughter was just a reminder of my previous marriage to Wendy.

I was not allowed to invite any guests to the house without her approval, and when I invited my parents over, Jennifer would make sure they left after an hour or so, making up lies to hurry them away.

My mother thought I had lost my mind. She thought the two of us living in that huge house was ludicrous. She'd bring food on her visits, but as soon as she left, Jennifer would toss it all down the garbage disposal.

"I don't like her cooking," she'd say, and that was that.

I was losing control of my life all over again. Allowing Jennifer to dictate to me made me feel small, like a servant, a kept husband. I had already given up too much for her. I had given up my life, really.

Eventually, I began to think about having an affair. I wanted a lover, someone in my life who loved and respected me for who I was. I wanted to touch and be touched. To feel passion, again.

I just wanted to be happy.

I had not found that with Wendy, and I knew from the beginning I would not find it with Jennifer, either. I had to do something.

I started making excuses to stay out late and go to the gay bars downtown. I drew attention in these bars because none of the regulars had seen me before. I'm sure they thought I was an out-of-town businessman just looking for a trick. Guys were hitting on me left and right and I loved the attention. The problem was that I couldn't take any of them home.

This practice became my outlet, my coping mechanism, a way to explore my true self and the life I desperately wanted to lead.

Attention from attractive men soothed my damaged ego and lifted my self-esteem. Often, I would think about Jacob -- how he was honest with himself and ultimately chose to do what made him happy. I so envied that life, that freedom, and wanted to emulate it.

Jennifer's mother had died shortly before we met, and her father George lived alone, about an hour away in Indiana. One Friday morning he called and asked if I had Cynthia that weekend. When I told him I did, he asked if he could come over for the weekend to see us, maybe help around the house a bit.

George was a wonderful man and he loved kids, and it was clear he'd been lonely since his wife passed away. So, of course I told him that we'd love to see him.

He arrived that afternoon and we ordered pizza and played games with Cynthia, who he adored, and just had a great time.

Around 7pm, I heard Jennifer come in through the garage and storm upstairs, slamming our bedroom door behind her. I chose to ignore her, but it was obvious to everyone that she was angry about something.

After a moment, we heard her voice on the house intercom.

"Can I see you upstairs, Patrick?" Jennifer announced.

I left George and Cynthia and went upstairs.

"What's the matter with you?" I asked.

"Is that my father downstairs?"

"Yes. What's the big deal?"

"Who invited him?"

"He's lonely. He called earlier and wanted to visit, so I said 'sure.'"

"I did not give you permission to invite him over."

I could hardly believe my ears. I was literally speechless.

"Go downstairs and tell him to leave," Jennifer demanded.

I had never stood up to Jennifer during our marriage, but this was too much. I resented her telling me what to do, how she always had to have her way, and I resented the fact that she was a huge part of my unhappiness. I had had it.

"No way!" I shouted.

She leered at me like I was a dog that had suddenly stood up on its hind legs and ordered a cocktail.

"What did you say to me?" she asked.

"If you want him gone, go tell him yourself," I said.

How could I be married to such a heartless bitch? Who treats her own father that way?

Jennifer demanded I leave the room and slammed the door behind me, locking it. I went back to the family room.

"Is Jennifer coming down?" asked George.

"No George, she's not feeling well and wants to go to bed," I said.

The next morning Jennifer came down to make breakfast, but she didn't speak a single word to me the rest of the weekend.

After that day she began to work late several nights a week, sometimes not getting home until after eleven at night. Sometimes she'd tell me to sleep in another bedroom because she didn't want me lying next to her.

I withdrew. I became distant with my friends and family. I was living a life most straight guys would love, in a big, expensive home with everything money could buy and a wife who no longer seemed to care what I did. But instead, I felt trapped.

It wasn't freedom she was giving me, it was a prison sentence.

When Jennifer was irritated with me, which now was most of the time, she wouldn't talk to me for days. She'd often come home and go straight up to the bedroom and lock the door. When I knocked, she'd scream that we had six other bedrooms in the house.

I didn't know how much longer I could deal with her crazed, erratic moods.

In my relationships with both Wendy and Jennifer, I ceded all control of my life to them. And they willingly took it. I allowed both women to abuse me verbally and emotionally. But why? What kept me so passive and unable to assert myself?

Was it because I was sexually-abused when I was nine years old? Did it have something to do with my family and how I related to them? Was it simply easier to allow my abusers to treat me like shit than to take control over the situation? By allowing the abuse, did that relieve me of my own guilt?

I came to realize that the relationships I chose forced me to act like some kind of machine, routinely going through the motions and never having to think for myself.

In the summer of 2001, Jennifer and I got into a huge argument and I stormed out of the house. When I returned that night, she apologized for her behavior and, rather un-expectantly, asked me to make love to her.

We had not had sex together for weeks.

I submitted, but was not at all into the sex and just wanted to get it over with. I had no interest in being with Jennifer at that time and, to this day, I'm not sure why I remained and allowed the intercourse to happen.

Days later, Jennifer asked me what I thought about having a baby.

I thought she had lost her mind.

"I *don't* think that's a good idea, Jennifer. You don't like kids, and our relationship... isn't the best right now."

That was putting a fine spin on it.

She looked at me for a moment and then said, "Patrick, I'm pregnant with your child."

I was stunned. "I thought you were on the pill."

"I went off a few months ago," she said.

I couldn't believe it.

"Did you ever think about telling me?" I said.

"I can do what I want," she said coldly. "It's my body."

"But it's *my* kid!" I yelled.

Unspoken here was that I was not sure it really was my child.

"It's not your concern, Patrick," Jennifer replied.

I felt like a sixteen year-old kid who'd just knocked up his girlfriend. When my friends and family found out about the pregnancy, they thought the same thing as I did - that the baby wasn't mine. It was clear at this point that Jennifer was playing a treacherous game with me, but I needed to be careful. Jennifer was a very smart woman. We went ahead and announced the news as if we had planned it all along.

Christmas Eve 2001, and Jennifer was four months pregnant. Cynthia got up early that morning to see what Santa had brought her. She came into our room and woke me up, excited about everything that awaited her that day.

I got up and took Cynthia downstairs so we wouldn't wake up Jennifer. After a while we heard doors opening and closing and assumed Jennifer would be coming down. When she didn't, I called her on the intercom and asked if she was coming down to open presents, but she didn't answer.

We waited for about an hour, and then I heard her high heels clacking on the stairs. Sure enough, a moment later I realized she was dressed for work.

"You're not going to work on Christmas Eve!" I said.

"I certainly am," said Jennifer.

Cynthia ran over to her and said, "But you have to see what Santa brought me!"

Jennifer looked down at her and said, "Spoiled brats like you don't deserve gifts from Santa."

Cynthia burst into tears and Jennifer just walked away.

I caught up to her as she got into her car. "If you *ever* talk to my daughter like that again, I will rip your head off."

She just backed out of the garage and left me standing there, furious.

I went back inside to console my daughter, and we gathered all her things and some of mine and went to my parents' house. I was gone the entire week, thinking about filing for divorce.

On New Year's Eve, I had Cynthia so I called my cousin Lisa and asked her if she and the kids wanted to stay at a hotel near the airport. It had an indoor pool and the kids could swim while we talked.

While we were there, Jennifer called my cell.

"Where are you? You haven't called all week," she said.

"We're at a hotel with my cousin and her kids," I told her.

"You're with Cynthia?"

"Of course."

There was a long pause, which, in Jennifer's case, means something. She's never at a loss for words and rarely has to take so long to decide how to proceed.

Finally, she spoke. "I need to ask you something."

"Go ahead," I said.

"You need to decide between me and Cynthia," she demanded.

"You've made that an easy decision, Jennifer," I said. "Cynthia, hands-down."

I felt so liberated and peaceful at that moment, the moment my daughter's name escaped my lips. Was Jennifer so clueless to think I would give up my life with my child? What kind of a person was she? Every time she said or did something crazy, I always thought that she'd outdone herself, but here was the latest surprise. I just couldn't comprehend how she would think I'd choose otherwise.

"It was nice knowing you," I said, and hung up.

My cousin Lisa heard this and asked me what happened. When I told her, all she could do was shake her head. "Is that bitch crazy?" she laughed.

I shook my head, as well.

"Patrick, I don't know how you find these people, but I hope you do better the next time," Lisa said.

"Me, too," I said.

"Cousin," she said, "all I want is for you to be happy and do what you want in life. Why is that so hard for you?"

That was a very important moment for me.

It was my chance to come clean, to finally tell someone in my family who loved me that I was gay and that I had been living a lie all these years, that I had been making decisions to please other people my entire life, and had never been honest about who I really was. Lisa would understand, wouldn't she? She would support me, wouldn't she?

The moment passed.

I couldn't do it. I was a coward. Instead, I told Lisa we were taking the kids to the most expensive restaurant in the hotel and that Jennifer would be picking up the tab.

Lisa just looked at me. "Cousin, I love you very much, but there is something wrong. I wish you would just tell me."

She was giving me *another* chance, and still I couldn't do it!

"Honey, I'm fine. I've just made some bad decisions in my life," I said.

Why couldn't I just tell her?

"Okay, Patrick. But you know I'm always here for you, right?"

"Of course," I told her.

There was so much more that I could have said at that moment, but that was how we left it.

I took the next few days off after the New Year. I wanted to think about how I was going to break things off with Jennifer. Telling her over the phone was one thing, reality was quite another. I needed to figure things out and be smart about it. Really smart.

I had been through an awful divorce with Wendy, who knew that I would do anything to keep joint custody of Cynthia and took full advantage of that fact. But I had the feeling Jennifer was going to make my life a living hell from here on out.

I discussed all of this with Mark, who had been right about so much, and he found an attorney for me.

Mary Larson was a very serious woman, and from what Mark told me, an excellent divorce attorney. I met with her the very next day and told her everything, from the rumors that Jennifer was having an affair to my fear that she was pregnant and of my suspicions that the child, if Jennifer *was* pregnant, was not even mine. I even told her about our sex life, which was, to be blunt, mostly inactive.

My attorney advised me to move back into the house immediately, which I did the following day.

Jennifer assumed we were going to patch things up, which was good news - for me, at least. It would be a lot better if she didn't know what I was doing until we actually filed for divorce, so I played it cool and just tried to keep things peaceful.

At the request of my attorney, while Jennifer was at work, I took an entire filing cabinet full of her financial records to my attorney's office and spent the whole day with her assistant making copies of everything.

A few days later, my attorney had divorce papers served at Jennifer's workplace, which, as you can imagine, enraged her. She called me screaming about how I was trying to take all her money and how she should have listened to her family and gotten a prenup.

Later that day, when my attorney called and told me she had a few questions for me, I mentioned how upset Jennifer was after getting served the divorce papers.

"She has good reason to be," she said.

"What do you mean?" I asked.

"Patrick, how many bank accounts did you have in your name before the marriage?"

"One account with First Chicago," I answered.

"How much money did you have in that account before the marriage?" she asked.

"About two thousand dollars, I guess."

"Did you and Jennifer open an account in your name after you got married?"

"No, why?" I said.

"Are you sure about that?" she asked.

"We did go to Jennifer's bank when we signed the mortgage papers," I said. "I think there was an account I signed for so she could use it for some inheritance money."

"Tell me about that one," she said.

"Jennifer's mother left her some money and she wanted to use that account to keep it separate or something. I didn't know how much it was and I didn't ask," I said.

"Why not?" she said.

"Didn't seem to be any of my business. What are you getting at?"

"Well, Patrick, your wife is a very smart woman, but she may have slipped up this time. She probably didn't want to pay the inheritance taxes."

"What does all this mean?" I asked.

"It means she put $200,000 dollars in a bank account with your name on it. *Only* your name. Which means, by law, the money is yours," she told me.

"That's Jennifer. Always surprising me," I said. "Mary, I can't take that money. It doesn't belong to me."

"Patrick, just let me handle things. I'll do what's right for you," she said.

Once the papers were filed, as I'd predicted, Jennifer did everything she could to make my life miserable. She took the car away, so I had to walk two miles to take the train into the city for work, and a hundred other things to irritate me. We lived separate lives in the house and avoided each other at all costs.

The house went on the market and sold within two months.

But in those two months, Jennifer did everything in her power to make me suffer. This was one of her strengths.

By the time of our divorce proceeding, Jennifer was six months pregnant. At that point she was ready to do anything to get me out of her life, and my attorney thought an agreement could be finalized if I asked for a paternity test.

"Have her prove the child is yours, Patrick," she said. "It's that simple."

Jennifer was in the living room watching the news that night when I brought it up. "I was talking to my attorney today and she had a good idea," I said.

Jennifer sneered. "What have *you* got to lose?"

"My attorney suggested you get a paternity test," I said.

Jennifer looked at me with revulsion in her eyes. "You listen to me, Patrick. If I get a paternity test and it's your child, I will drain you of every last cent you have in this world. In the state of Illinois, it makes no difference how much money the wife has; the man pays twenty percent of his salary. Between me and Wendy, that's half your miserable income, you pathetic loser!"

I couldn't believe I ever got involved with this insufferable woman. And she wasn't through, either.

"Once this child is born, don't think you'll have it easy, either. I'll make sure you suffer every time you visit!" she shouted.

"Is that what you want for your child, Jennifer?" I asked.

"Don't fight me on this, Patrick, I'm serious. If you fight me, I'll make every day you wake up another day you wish you were dead!" she declared.

Why was I allowing her to push me around like this?

The truth was I was worried that if the baby was mine, I wouldn't be able to support my kids and myself. I knew Jennifer was serious about making my life miserable if I pursued this issue, and I knew that would adversely affect the child.

These feelings again brought me back to the rape when I was a child. I felt trapped, with no way out, and this person had full control of me. I felt weak and again felt myself giving in to the habit of putting others' needs and demands before my own.

Once the house sold, I had to move out. I went back to live with my parents. I was lucky I had parents that loved me, although at this point they certainly didn't understand me.

As painful as it is to admit it, Jennifer was right about one thing: without her, I was broke and could barely support Cynthia and myself.

A month before we went to court, Jennifer had the baby. She didn't tell me until a week later, in an email she sent me at work.

"On May 2, 2002, I gave birth to a healthy baby boy I named Peter Draper," she wrote. "I thought you might want to know before we went to court."

That was it. I'm not sure whether it was a courtesy or a warning.

At that point, Jennifer had moved and failed to provide me with any forwarding address.

In the days leading up to our court date, I was torn, not at all sure what I was going to do. My attorney again encouraged me to demand the paternity test.

The thing is, I knew Jennifer might be telling me the truth and that there was a chance, however slim, that Peter was mine. If he was and I forced Jennifer to prove it, I had no doubt she would make both our lives miserable.

What it boiled down to was that Jennifer wanted to keep her money and her baby, and if I allowed her that, she would leave me alone.

The divorce was settled in June of 2002. I was granted visitation and money, but the money would be awarded as pre-child support for Peter. Jennifer agreed to stay in the state of Illinois.

I verbally agreed with Jennifer that I would not seek to visit Peter in the future.

I have never been the same after that divorce. I often think about the son I may have given up, the son I will very likely never know. It hurts to think of him out there, not knowing whether he's mine, and to think of Cynthia having no idea she might have a brother.

I kept asking myself why I was such a coward. Why I again allowed an abusive person to take control over my life.

Why don't I ever fight back?

In 2004, I discovered that Jennifer had taken a position at her company's office as president of the southeast region and relocated to Orlando without telling me, in direct violation of our divorce decree. I also discovered she was living with her ex-boss, the same man she'd been having an affair with for years. Apparently he'd left his wife and kids, and was now living with Jennifer and Peter.

Recently, I tried searching for her and Peter again, but had no luck. The records I found do not show them in Florida any longer, and Jennifer no longer works for that company. It's like they disappeared off the face of the earth.

I've thought of hiring a private investigator to look for them, but even if I did find them, I'd still be faced with the same situation as before: Forcing Jennifer to prove whether or not Peter is my son.

I want to know the truth, but I don't want to disrupt Peter's life. I lived through a custody battle with Wendy, and it would hurt too much to relive that experience. I know Jennifer would be worse than Wendy.

Maybe Cynthia and I will find out about Peter one day. Maybe when he's older, he'll want to find us. It will be difficult, because he doesn't even have our last name on his birth certificate. But, I have faith. I think about him all the time and pray every day that he's safe and that, somehow, he knows that I love him.

If I could look in his eyes just one time, maybe feel the touch of his hand in mine, I think I would know the truth. Until my dying day, I will pray that happens.

Chapter 9 (2002 – 2004)
Man of My Dreams

After all the heartache I'd experienced with Jennifer, I was determined to live my life on my own terms from now on.

I was ready for a fresh start, and I knew I was done having relationships with women.

Being married to two controlling and demanding women had taken a toll on my psyche. I felt almost as if I needed to be cleansed, stripped of my prior life and immersed in that part of me I had so long denied before the world.

I was ready to take charge of my life.

Being extremely curious about gay life but knowing so little about it really scared me. The unknown can be both exciting and frightening at the same time.

Still, I was drawn to it like a moth to the flame.

I'd visited gay bars in the past, of course, but it had been a while.

I decided that if I was going to give this a try, I had to do it my way. Though I had only been separated from Jennifer for a few months, I wanted adventure. I wanted to be free.

One Saturday afternoon in July of 2002, I just decided to go for it.

I was a gay man and I wasn't going to hide it any longer!

I grabbed my roller blades and headed to Boystown. It was a

beautiful summer day as I skated along the lakefront, wearing only gym shorts, sunglasses, and a headband.

After a couple of hours, my body was glistening in the afternoon sun, and I noticed quite a few attractive guys checking me out as I passed them.

Their eyes felt wonderful on my body, which was fit and toned. I also looked pretty cute. I could tell they wanted me, and it made me feel incredibly sensuous.

I wanted to feel desired; I needed it. I knew some of that was due to my low self-esteem, but I didn't care. Showing off my body and imagining those men imagining me gave me tremendous pleasure.

I skated across Lake Shore Drive onto Aldine Street and suddenly ran into a man getting out of a cab. The poor guy had his hands full with bags from Nordstrom's, Marshall Field's, and other trendy shops. Those bags flew in every direction upon our sudden impact.

I landed on top of him in the grass, and the first thing I noticed was the deep blue of his eyes and his rugged, masculine chin. He was dressed in white linen pants and a polo shirt under a blue blazer.

It was as if I'd plunged head-first into a romantic comedy, and this was the 'meet-cute.'

"I'm so sorry!" I said. "Are you okay?"

He smiled and my heart melted. "Just a few dented boxes."

"It was all my fault," I said. "I can go pretty good on the blades but I have problems stopping."

He laughed and stood up. The sun shone behind him, giving the illusion of a golden halo, and then my angel reached out his hand.

"Up you go," he said, and up I went. His hand was cool and firm in mine, and it felt good. It felt right.

"I'm so sorry," I repeated, and he just laughed again and told me not to worry.

That lively encounter might have ended there had the man not taken out his business card. "May I give you this?" he asked.

"Why on earth would you want to do that?" I asked, genuinely surprised.

"You knocked me down," he answered. "The least you could do is buy me a drink."

For some reason, all of my newfound confidence drained out of me, and I blurted out, "But, I'm not gay."

He just laughed. "Call me," he said. "You owe me a beer."

I'm not sure if the embarrassment showed on my face since I was already red from the sun, but I felt like such a fool for saying that. '*But, I'm not gay.*'

He must think that I think **he's** gay! Is he? Aren't I?

It was all very confusing.

Thank God I managed to just say, "Thanks, I'll give you a call."

After we parted company, the excitement took over. I was so happy to have met such a seemingly nice guy, and in such a peculiar way, too! We weren't at a bar or social event. We literally ran into each other on the street. Or, I should say, I ran into him.

I went home and had dinner with my folks, but I wasn't really *there* at all. I was back on the street, crashing into Prince Charming over and over. I could not get this guy out of my head.

Why didn't I say this? Why didn't I say that? I felt like I was back in high school.

The anticipation was killing me, so I decided to call him that very night. I know how that sounds, too eager and all that. But I couldn't wait. I know I was acting on impulse, since I had barely spent five minutes in this man's presence. But if that meet-up happened like that because I was meant to spend the rest of my life with that man, I wanted the rest of my life to start as soon as possible.

I called him around ten, thinking I could just leave a message. The phone rang three times and I nearly hung up, but then he answered and my heart stopped for a moment.

"Hello, anyone there?" he said.

"Yes," I said. "I mean, I'm looking for Marty."

"This is he."

It's now or never. I can hang up or I can tell him who I am and see where this leads. Wait! Does he recognize my voice? If he does and I hang up, I can never call him again! Too embarrassing!

"This is Patrick!" I blurted. "We ... ran into each other today."

"I thought that was you!" he said, sounding pleased.

He recognized my voice!

We talked for a while, getting to know each other a bit, and I'd like to relay some of our conversation here, but everything was such a blur until Marty actually asked me out.

"What are you doing tomorrow afternoon?" he asked.

"I don't have any plans," I said, trying to act cool as my heart nearly beat out of my chest.

How does he not hear that?

"Let's meet outside the building where you nearly killed me today," he said.

I laughed. He certainly had a way with words.

"Sure," I said.

"One o'clock? We can grab some lunch."

I must have said 'yes', but by that time I was so giddy I was almost levitating.

I didn't get a wink of sleep that night.

The next day was Sunday. I dressed in shorts, gym shoes, and a tank top. I was pleased that I'd been shirtless when we met, so he knew what I looked like. I wanted him to see me like that again.

Marty showed up looking good in golf shorts, a golf shirt, and tennis shoes. I thought we made a fine pair. We went to lunch at a café on Broadway, a few blocks from his place, and talked and laughed the entire afternoon.

Before we knew it, it was six in the evening! The day flew by so quickly, I was actually shocked when I noticed the time. I walked Marty back to his building, and the entire way there I was nervous as hell.

What would I say to him when we got to his door?

He saved me again. As soon as we arrived, he turned to me and said, "Can I kiss you goodnight?"

I'm lucky my knees didn't buckle. I was so nervous and excited, I'm surprised I got the word out of my mouth, but I'm so glad I did.

"Sure," I said.

I'll never forget that moment, the moment our lips touched for the first time. I distinctly remember his lips being smooth and supple, and wondering if mine were the same. I remember his arms pulling me close. His cologne. His body close to mine.

The kiss seemed to last forever.

When I stepped back, he asked me if everything was okay. He could obviously sense that I was nervous.

"Sure," I said. "I just have to get up early for work."

"Can I call you?" he said.

Even after such a great first date, I was a little scared and reluctant to give him my business card, but he seemed like such a great guy that I couldn't refuse.

Refuse? Was I crazy?

Marty called me at work the next day and asked if he could take me to dinner the following Saturday. I had not told him about Cynthia and how she was scheduled to spend the next, entire weekend with me.

"I'm sorry, Marty, but I can't this weekend," I said.

"Are you playing hard to get?" he asked.

"No, I just have plans with my family."

"How about Thursday, then?"

Yes!

He offered to pick me up, but that wasn't going to happen since I was living with my parents.

"How about I meet you there?" I said.

"I'll email you the address before Thursday," he said.

He was so easygoing!

"Sounds good," I said.

"See you on Thursday, handsome," Marty said.

Marty looked stunning on Thursday in a blue pinstripe suit with red tie and a red handkerchief.

"You look great!" I said, and he leaned in and kissed me on the cheek. Dinner was wonderful. We ate, drank wine, and talked and talked.

He told me he was from Philadelphia and that his parents still lived there. I gave him an abbreviated version of my family story, leaving out the details I thought might scare him away.

After dinner Marty offered to drive me home, but I had driven myself. I walked him down the street and we kissed passionately next to his car, which was parked on Halsted Street. I wasn't nearly as nervous as I was earlier, both because of the wine and because Halsted is the main 'gay street' in the city; gay couples holding hands and kissing is not an uncommon sight along that boulevard.

"Can I see you again next week?" he asked.

"That would be great," I replied.

During the entire week before our next date, we spoke on the phone twice a day. It seemed so natural and right. I never thought I could be in that place with another man.

The next Friday, Marty made a dinner reservation for us at the Capitol Grill, an upscale 'steak and chops' restaurant where Jennifer and I would go for her work dinners. I was excited to see him because it had almost been a week since our last meeting.

The day before our date I went shopping. I wanted to look special for Marty.

I was tired of all the boring clothes that Jennifer had me wear. I had to be conservative during the day for work, but I wanted to look sexy for our big night out on the town.

Except for a poolside incident in Hawaii and the day I ran into Marty, I never thought I could be sexy, but he made me feel confident. I had allowed Wendy and Jennifer to mold me into the husband they wanted me to be. I allowed my family to mold me into the son they wanted me to be. This was my chance to be who *I* really wanted to be.

I went up to Halsted Street to a clothing store that catered to gay men. When I walked in, I spotted a very cute salesman who looked about twenty-one. I could tell he thought I was some straight guy from out of town who had accidentally stumbled into his gay men's store.

He looked me up and down. "Is there anything in particular you're looking for?" he asked.

I was kind of startled, because at that moment I really wasn't sure what I was looking for.

"I need an outfit for a special date," I said.

He looked me up and down again. "Mister, are you sure this is the right store for you?"

"I think so," I replied.

He leaned in close and whispered, "This is a *gay* men's clothing store."

I took a deep breath. "This isn't easy for me to say, but tomorrow I have a date with a good-looking guy, and I really want to look sexy."

He took a step back and looked me over again.

"I would never have figured *you* to be gay," he said.

I wasn't sure whether or not that was a compliment, but I smiled and asked if he could help.

"Girlfriend, I am going to fix you up," he declared.

I followed that cute guy all through the store. First we looked at jeans. He pulled out a pair with sparkles on them.

"No way," I said. "I'll do tight, but nothing that looks like girls' jeans."

He smiled knowingly. "I hear what you're saying, tough guy. I have just the outfit for you."

He pulled some tight-fitting black jeans with an etched design on the back pockets, and then selected a stylish, white dress shirt with a black sports jacket to go over it.

As I was paying for the clothes, he asked, "Can I give you one more tip?"

"Of course," I said.

He recommended that I pick up this sticky hair product at the salon next door. "You have nice hair, but I think with this outfit, you need to spike it up some."

"Thanks, I really appreciate it," I said.

"What's your name, tough guy?" he asked.

"Patrick," I said.

"Well Patrick, my name is Randy, and any time you need something, you come back and visit me," he said.

I told him I would. And, eventually, I did. Randy was a lot younger than me but it was obvious that he was completely comfortable with who he was, and that was exactly where I wanted to be, as well.

I was scheduled to meet Marty for dinner that Friday night at the Capitol Grill, but when I got home from work, my parents were already eating dinner. "Honey, I made some pasta and meatballs for you, sit down and eat it before it gets cold," Mom said.

"Mom, I have plans tonight," I said.

"Plans? With who?" she asked.

"Some friends from work."

"Who?"

"Mark and the guys."

"Please don't be home late," she said. "I worry about you."

"Mom, I've been married *twice*," I said. "I lived away from home for over eight years!"

"Exactly my point," she said. "You stayed out late with *those* two and look where it got you!"

She never lets up.

"Mom, I'm a grown man," I said, exasperated, before retiring to my apartment in the basement. I got dressed and departed through the back door so she wouldn't see my outfit.

As I left, Mom shouted after me, "Call if you're going to be out late!"

I ran for the bus to take me downtown. I was so happy to be seeing Marty.

When I walked into the Capitol Grill, it was filled with striking, well-dressed couples.

The host asked, "Do you have a reservation?"

"I'm meeting Marty Jack," I said.

The man looked up and smiled. "He's been waiting for you."

Right then I knew the host was gay and he knew we were on a date.

Marty was seated on the opposite end of the room, and he

watched me approvingly as I made my way through the elegant, spacious restaurant. I felt like Brad Pitt, everyone's eyes fixed on me as I passed by their tables. Marty had a bottle of champagne chilling in a bucket of ice. It was perfect.

Marty stood up, handed me a single, long-stemmed rose, and kissed me on the cheek. "You look fantastic, honey," he said.

"*This* old outfit?" I teased.

We sat down and Marty poured us a glass of champagne. "I'm so proud to be here with you tonight, Patrick," he declared.

"I'm happy to be here, handsome." I had never said that to a man before, but it felt natural saying it to Marty. I felt like I was living the dream I had dreamt all my life.

After a while, I finally got the nerve to tell Marty things I hadn't yet shared with him. I knew if this thing was going to move forward, he needed to know more of my history.

I told Marty I was divorced and had a six year-old daughter. And as always, I had a full complement of photos in my wallet, which I shared with him.

"Such a pretty little girl," he said. "You're very lucky, Patrick."

He wasn't kidding.

Marty told me he had always wanted kids but felt it would never happen. He took the news of Cynthia very well, but I was not yet ready to tell him everything. My life was almost too much for *me* to handle. I was afraid that if I shared too much, too soon Marty would bound for the exit.

"I'm not normally a bar person," he said after dinner, "but how would you like to go to Sidetrack's for an after-dinner drink?"

Sidetrack was, and still is, a very popular gay club in Boystown. We jumped into a cab and took off for Halsted Street moments later. Once in the cab, Marty put his hand over mine and leaned over to kiss my ear. I smiled and he squeezed tighter, like he was telling me everything was okay.

This was the fantasy I had been waiting for my entire life, and it couldn't have been with a greater guy.

When we got to the club, it was jam-packed with a line out the door.

"Follow me," Marty said, and we walked to the front of the line, where the doorman stopped us.

"Back of the line, guys," he said.

Marty pulled out a fifty and stuffed it in the doorman's coat pocket.

"Right this way, gentlemen," he countered.

I felt secure and happy at that moment. All of my deep-seated insecurities suddenly vanished. We were seated at a table in the main bar, which was simply amazing; dramatic, steep walls with a glass ceiling, and more video screens than I could count, all playing dizzying music videos.

Marty ordered us a bottle of champagne, and we fit right in with the exclusive scene. There were scores of attractive guys of all type; young queens, older distinguished men, debonair professionals, and lots of good-looking men in our age-group.

People were dancing and singing and having fun. This is what I imagined gay life to be. At one point, I had to use the men's room and asked Marty to point me in the right direction.

"I think it's back that way," he said, but when I started to leave the table, he pulled me back and kissed me.

"I'll be right back," I assured him.

My walk to the restroom proved interesting. I passed a group of guys who gave me a quick and favorable appraisal. One of them said, "You're new around here! Stop and talk to us!"

I smiled and kept walking. I had everything I wanted back at my table. I felt very secure in my element.

The urinals in the bathroom were stainless steel with no partitions. I stood in a way so as to avoid exposing myself, but it wasn't easy.

As I washed my hands, two young guys appeared from one of the stalls, still making out.

This place was really something!

When I got back to the table, Marty asked if everything was okay.

"This is just all so new to me," I said.

"Not all gay people live like this, Patrick," he said. "I just wanted you to experience what club life is like."

After about an hour, Marty asked if I wanted to come back to his place. I thought it was a little quick and bold of him, but said, "Sure, why not?"

We walked back to Lake Shore Drive and up Aldine Street holding hands.

"Mr. Dati, you've really impressed me. I'm so glad we met."

"Marty, you've made me feel like a different person the past few weeks, and that's a very good thing," I assured him.

When we got to his building, the doorman opened the door and said, "Good evening, Mr. Jack."

"Good evening, Bill."

I was impressed that Marty had a doorman, and everything else was elegant, too, including his condo. The furniture was very traditional, but the interior design was very masculine.

I sat down on a plush sofa.

"How about a martini?" Marty asked. When he left the room to mix our drinks, I scratched his cat's ears and looked at the many pictures of his family throughout the living room. They all looked very distinguished and successful.

Why that mattered to me, I can't say.

Was being associated with wealthy people yet another issue I needed to confront? Was I ashamed of my modest upbringing?

At that moment, I wasn't sure of anything except that I was with a handsome man and his place felt warm and cozy.

Marty came back, handed me my drink and turned on some soft jazz. We sat and looked at each other for a moment, and then began to kiss.

"Would you like to spend the night?" he said.

I didn't say anything at first. I just kept kissing him. But it was obvious to us both what was going to happen.

"Yes," I whispered, and kissed his neck.

He broke away and said, "Excuse me for one minute." He left for a moment, and then summoned me into his bedroom.

When I entered the room it was lined with lit candles. It was like a scene from a romantic movie, flickering candles everywhere.

Could tonight be any more perfect?

Marty slowly undressed me and whispered, "Get under the covers," which I did.

Then he undressed for me and I saw him naked for the first time. He had a beautiful, muscular body, which would have looked amazing with or without the candlelight.

I wanted to sleep with him, but sex was not my goal that night. I wanted to see if our first night together could be more than that.

It was. The night was enchanting. We touched and kissed for an hour and eventually fell asleep in each other's arms. When I woke up the next morning Marty was not in bed, but I could smell fresh coffee and toast. I just lay there and enjoyed the feel of the soft sheets against my skin, remembering our perfect night together.

Marty entered the bedroom in a white bathrobe, carrying a tray with hot coffee and toasted bagels, and we enjoyed breakfast in bed.

"Thank you for last night, Marty," I said.

"It was my pleasure, Patrick. You're the best date I've had in years," he replied.

I gazed at him for a moment. "And thanks for not forcing me to do something I wasn't ready to do."

"Mr. Dati, this is not a one night stand," he said. "I see so much more for us in the future." Then, I kissed him.

When I left his place that morning and turned on my phone, there were a dozen messages from my mother.

My mother!

She answered on the first ring.

"What's up, Mom?" I asked casually.

"You haven't been home all night, Patrick. I was worried sick!" she complained.

"I told you I was out with my friends, Mom. We were drinking." I hated lying to my mother, and felt guilty.

Why did I feel guilty, though? It was my life and I was a grown man. Well, I felt guilty because she was my mom, and I didn't want to hurt her.

I told her Mark and I had too much to drink and so I slept over.

"That Mark is a good boy, I like him," she said.

If she knew the truth it would crush her, so I needed to continue the facade, I thought.

The next day was Sunday, and Marty called to ask me out to the movies. We had another delightful day. After the movie, we had lunch out, and Marty started to tell me more about his business. He traveled a lot and spent a few days a month in Miami and New York. He had two homes in Miami and liked to escape and relax in the sun at least once a month.

"Why don't we go down there next week?" he asked.

"That sounds great," I said, "but I can't afford to take a trip right now."

"Are you kidding?" he said. "I don't expect you to pay! Come on, it'll be fun. I have a pool and the ocean is right behind my high-rise."

Marty needed to go to Miami for a meeting on Wednesday and suggested I fly down and meet him on Friday evening. I wanted to go so badly, but what would I tell my parents?

"Can I tell you tomorrow?" I asked.

"Sure, that's fine," he said.

I thought about it all night. What was I going to tell my mother? I would have to lie again. I hated to lie, but I wanted to be with Marty so badly.

Why did I have to feel so guilty about just living life on my own terms?

It seemed like whatever made me happy, also made me feel guilty. I just didn't know how to be comfortable with myself. If I couldn't accept myself, how could I be open with my family?

I finally decided to tell Mom I had a business trip and needed to be out of town that weekend.

The following Friday, Marty sent a limo to pick me up at work and take me to the airport. When I boarded the plane, I realized he'd bought me a first class ticket! I'd never flown first class before. It was so nice sitting with rich people, drinking champagne and being treated like a V.I.P.

When we landed, there was a guy near the baggage area holding a sign with my name on it. "Mr. Dati, I'm your driver," he said. "I'll be taking you to Mr. Jack's residence."

I thought I was dreaming. The limo had a full bar and the driver told me to help myself to whatever I wanted. I was like a kid in a candy store. Before I went totally crazy, I called my mom to tell her I landed safely and everything was fine.

As soon as I hung up, my cell phone rang. It was Marty.

"I'm at home waiting to take you to dinner," he said.

We pulled up to a huge high-rise which fronted the marina, and, just as Marty had said, backed up against the ocean. The doorman greeted me by name and told me to take the elevator to the 18th floor. "I'll have your bags brought up shortly, Mr. Dati," he said.

I remember wondering what I'd done to deserve all this. Could I finally be happy? *Was Marty the man who would change my life?*

Marty was in the doorway waiting with open arms. We stood in the hallway hugging and kissing for so long that the bags arrived before we'd even moved an inch.

I was wowed beyond belief. I felt like I'd walked into an episode of *Lifestyles of the Rich and Famous*. His condo was stunning, very modern, with windows from floor to ceiling. Marty pressed a button in the living room and the drapes opened automatically onto a wonderful view of Miami Beach and the marina.

There was a beautifully wrapped gift box on the living room table. He picked it up and said, "I saw this and thought you should have it."

It was a black Giorgio Armani suit with a white shirt and multi-colored tie.

"Babe, you didn't have to buy me this," I said.

"Tomorrow I have a business meeting with my biggest client in Miami," Marty said. "And I told her all about you. She wants to meet you and I wanted you to have something special to wear. If it doesn't fit, my tailor will fix it in the morning."

I had never been in a relationship where someone treated me so special and did not abuse me. It was a wonderful feeling.

We went out on the town that night, and Miami was spectacular, filled with gorgeous people. We went to the Delano Hotel, which apparently was *the* place to be.

In Miami, people seemed to act how they wanted to, and I fit right in. Marty and I walked into the hotel arm in arm, and it didn't faze me because I didn't know anyone there. It felt safe to express myself as a gay man in this place.

That night we didn't get home until very late, and we were both aching with passion. We made love all night. It felt perfect with Marty. He never made me feel uncomfortable or made me do anything I didn't want to do.

He truly cared about me for who I was, and appeared to have no intentions of hurting me. I felt safe and in control of my life when I was with him.

We woke up the next day and went down to the pool. Marty had his own cabana with a full bar and private bathroom, and we hung out and swam and drank champagne. It was a short walk to the beach, and the weather was perfect. We walked hand in hand along the beach, and I felt like this was *it*. Marty was the one, the complete package. He was wealthy, handsome, and charming, and treated me like gold.

After hanging out on the beach all day, we went back to the condo and fell asleep in each other's arms.

Marty woke me up with a kiss later that afternoon. "Babe, we need to get ready for dinner," he said.

We took a luxurious shower together and it all felt so natural. I truly had never felt so comfortable with another person. Marty always made me feel good about myself.

I was a little nervous about the dinner with Marty's big client, though. I wanted desperately to make a good impression. We entered the swanky restaurant arm in arm, me in my brand-new Armani suit. We looked like a power couple.

My ex-wife, Jennifer, was a very powerful businesswoman.

But I never felt this way about us, because Jennifer did not share power. She kept it for herself. When I was with Jennifer, I felt like a trophy-husband being paid to be with her. Actually, I guess I *was* being paid to be with her.

Marty's client, Carol, was already seated as we approached holding hands. Carol stood up and kissed Marty on the cheek, and then looked at me. "Now, can I kiss this handsome man next to you?" she said.

We had a wonderful dinner and Marty and Carol talked a little business, but Marty never ignored me, interrupting their conversation every so often, explaining, 'my guy needs some attention.'

The way Marty made me feel was different from any other relationship I'd had before in my life. He paid attention to me, and cared about my feelings. He was not out to *get* anything from me, or control my life. He just wanted me in his life, and for us to be happy together.

When we returned from Miami the next weekend, I had Cynthia. Marty was dying to meet her and asked if he could join us that Saturday. I wasn't sure about this at first but decided to go with it, anyway. If Marty was going to be a part of my life, these two would have to meet eventually.

I brought Cynthia over to Marty's place, and we took her over to Navy Pier. The three of us rode the giant Ferris wheel and later went shopping at the pier's Build-A-Bear Workshop, where you can make your own teddy bear. Marty bought Cynthia a bear that she dressed up herself at the store. It was a sweet gift.

Over the next few weeks, Marty and I spent more and more time with Cynthia, and she eventually grew quite fond of Marty. I was ecstatic because Cynthia is my world, and if she didn't fit well with someone I brought into my life, that relationship could never last. That much was made clear from my time spent with Jennifer.

Marty had a business trip to New York planned that August, and I took a few extra days off for a long weekend together in the Big Apple. We stayed at the famous Waldorf Astoria, and on Saturday we rented roller blades because Marty wanted to skate through different New York neighborhoods in honor of our unusual first encounter.

We skated across Central Park and then took a limo to the Brooklyn Bridge. We skated through Chelsea, and finally ended up in Greenwich Village for a late lunch.

How often do you get a chance to rollerblade through all the great neighborhoods of New York City? It was like one of those impossibly romantic New York days you see in movie montages.

With Marty it was always, "Whatever makes you happy, honey."

He was my romantic ideal, almost too good to be true.

After returning from New York, Marty told me his parents were coming into town to visit. He was not very excited by this news because his mother tended to weigh on his nerves. But Marty really wanted me to meet them, anyway. "I want them to meet the guy that rocks my world," he declared.

The strange thing is that I had still not mentioned Marty to anyone I knew. I was just living this wonderful dream but not telling anyone about it. It made me feel safe that I didn't have to worry about what my family thought of us. Marty seemed to understand this and didn't pressure me about it. "It will happen when the time is right," he said.

We took Marty's parents to The Ritz-Carlton for brunch, and I could tell his mother was already trying his nerves. To me, she just seemed to be a mother asking me questions, but it annoyed Marty all the same.

After brunch I insisted Marty spend some time alone with his parents, in spite of his protests. Marty's parents lived in Philadelphia and didn't get to see him all that often.

As I was getting into a cab, he told me, "You're making me the happiest man in the world."

The feeling was mutual, to say the least.

After that, things started to get more serious between us. One night in bed Marty held me in his arms and told me he was falling in love with me. I wasn't sure what to say. There was no doubt in my mind that I was feeling the same way, but I was scared to actually say the words.

"Is something wrong?" he asked.

I gathered my courage. "I love you, too," I said.

In spite of my hesitation, everything about that moment felt right.

This was it. I was finally living the life I had always hoped for. I met someone who loved and respected me. Someone who didn't try to control me, or demean me with vicious insults. Marty loved me for who I was. There was nothing about me he would not accept, I felt.

But, why had I waited so long for this moment? Was it just God's way of telling me to walk down the path before I could run?

Over the next few weeks, I had family obligations and could not spend as much time with Marty. He began to ask about meeting my family. He knew I wasn't 'out' to them, and he seemed okay with that. He just wanted to meet and get a feel for them. Especially since he'd heard so many colorful stories about them. How could he *not* be curious?

I told Marty he'd be in for a shock, but he willingly accepted the challenge.

One Sunday, my dad and Marco were at home watching football while Mom cooked dinner. I asked Mom if I could invite a friend over to join us for dinner, and she said, "Any friend of yours is welcome in this home." This is something she'd often say to me.

I was apprehensive, but then Marty appeared very straight, so I figured my parents would never figure that we were lovers. Marty arrived and I took him into the kitchen. Mom was at the stove making pasta and meatballs, and Dad was sitting with Marco at the kitchen table, watching the Bears game.

I introduced Marty to everyone, and he handed my mother a bottle of red wine and a lovely bouquet of flowers. Mom loved that. None of my other friends ever brought my mother flowers like that, but then she had no idea how Marty figured in my life.

Marco shook hands and got Marty a beer. Marty then sat down with my dad and Marco to watch the game. He knew my father had been ill and was very solicitous of Dad's state of health. Later on, after Marty had left, my mother said, "I really like your friend. How did you boys meet?"

I lied and said that we met through my friend Mark, and that we were both rollerbladers.

"Well, he's a very nice gentleman," Mom said.

Marty was delighted that things went so well that night. He had no judgmental comments of any kind, and was very accepting of my family because he loved me and knew that I loved them. This was such a contrast from Wendy and Jennifer, both of whom resented my strong commitment to family. Neither one of them could ever understand how my family really *lived* for one another. It didn't make sense to either of them that this was simply the way we all grew up. My family had strong values, and we watched out for each other.

Marty and I were spending several nights a week together and, at one point, he asked me to move in with him.

I reflected back upon a day my imagination ran wild with this very fantasy. It had all seemed so far-fetched back then, but now here was Marty proposing that very reality.

"It's too soon," I said. "I need to think about it."

"Take a few days," he said, as always, loving and thoughtful. Part of me wanted to say 'yes' right away; the other part of me was thinking only about my family.

What would they think? And what about Cynthia? Would she understand?

Once again, I couldn't focus on my life because I was too concerned about what everyone else would think.

Here, I had the chance to be the person I was born and meant to be, but I was too worried about the effect it would have upon my family and friends.

Why did I care? Why couldn't I just be happy in the moment and live my life as I wanted?

A few days later, I gave Marty my decision. "I love you and want to be with you, but I'm just not ready for us to move in together," I said.

Marty told me we could find an apartment near his so we could spend more time together. I thought this was a perfect idea. I could be with Marty in my gay life and still hold on to my straight life, and no one had to know. I had allowed my family so much control over me that I could not move in with the man I loved. Maybe I was also afraid that if I moved in with him, I would lose control over my life once again.

Over the next few months, Marty and I were inseparable. We spent ample time with Cynthia and I joined him on his business trips to New York and Miami. It was thrilling to explore those two cities together. We were like two teenagers in love, and when we were away from Chicago, I didn't care what the world thought.

But at home I was still living a lie, and that kind of life ultimately has to come to an end.

Marty always treated me like a king, or maybe I should say 'queen.' What did it matter? We were in love!

It all felt very natural for me, but I went through episodes of guilt because my family started to wonder why I was not around as much anymore. And I had to lie to them. It felt awful because I was so happy and in love with Marty that I just naturally wanted to share that with all the other people I loved. I wanted them to know about Marty, but I felt sworn to secrecy.

As time went on, Marty could tell I was really struggling. He tried to tell me that, in time, my family would learn to accept our relationship, but that only made me feel more anxious. I was scared out of my mind because even though I really loved him, I felt like I could never be out as a gay man. I started to feel like I was leading Marty on, lying to my family, and being untrue to who I really was.

Something had to give.

I started to spend more time with my family and making excuses as to why I couldn't see Marty - and it was driving him nuts. I was avoiding him and we both knew it.

Why was I doing this? Marty made me feel like I had never felt before. Why was I pulling away from someone who loved me and made me feel so safe?

One Sunday morning, Marty called and said he needed to see me. I told him that I couldn't come by because I was taking my mother to church and then spending the afternoon with my family, but he was adamant. I agreed to see him, and later went over to his place. We were walking to the coffee shop when he took my hand. But I pulled it away.

"I can't," I said. "I'm sorry, but I can't."

"Can't what?" Marty asked. "Patrick Dati, I love you and want to spend our life together. I am not either of your ex-wives. I am not going to hurt you. Please let it go."

I started to cry. I couldn't even look at him. He grabbed me and said, "It's going to be okay. We're going to get through this together."

I just stared at the ground.

"Damn it, Patrick, let me into your life," he said. "Why do you shut down when someone wants to love you?"

I finally spoke up. "Babe, I love you, but I cannot live my life as a gay man. My family means too much to me and I can't just walk away from them."

Now Marty was crying. "Don't do this to us," he pleaded.

I cried in his arms and then pushed him away. "I have to go," I said.

"You're breaking my heart, Patrick," he said.

"You'll find someone else," I said.

"I don't *want* anyone else! I want you, Patrick Dati."

My heart seemed to stop beating, a feeling I'd never experienced before.

I was walking away from the man of my dreams, though part of me thought I was doing the right thing: I was doing it for my family.

A few months went by, and it was now March of 2004. Marty

and I had not communicated, but both of us had a birthday coming up, so I called him at his office.

"I totally understand if you don't want to talk to me, Marty, but I wanted to see how you were doing," I said.

"I miss you," he said.

"Our birthdays are both coming up," I said. "Maybe we could have drinks."

"I'd love that," Marty said.

We met at our favorite spot, the Capitol Grill.

Marty looked amazing, just like on our first date. He ordered a bottle of wine and we had a wonderful dinner. Marty asked me to come back to his house, and I agreed. The truth was that I wanted to feel him again. I wanted to be touched by him like before.

He'd decorated for my birthday and a huge gift was sitting on the sofa. I was overwhelmed by his generosity and honest love for me. I had previously been married to two women and neither had ever made me feel so loved. There was really no comparison.

We spent the rest of the weekend together and it was magical. Just like it had been in the beginning. I wasn't sure how the weekend would end, or if I even wanted it to.

Sunday evening eventually arrived, and as we sat on the sofa looking deeply into each other's eyes, Marty popped the question.

"Patrick, I love you and want to spend the rest of my life with you. Will you be my partner?"

I had a feeling that this was going to come up, but thought Marty would wait a few days until everything had sunk in. "I need an answer before you leave tonight," he said.

What was I doing? What could I say?

I was overwhelmed. "Marty, I love you and can imagine spending my life with you, but I can't answer that question tonight."

He started to cry.

"Please don't be upset," I said.

"Patrick, you told me about how you were raped as a child, and about all the problems you've suffered since. Is that keeping us apart? Is that why you can't love?"

I went silent for several minutes. *But I can love. Can't I?*

"Why can't we give it some time, Marty?" I asked. "I just need a little more time."

"If you loved me, nothing else would matter," he said, tears streaming down his face. "Can you please just go?"

"Marty, I need you in my life!" I cried.

"Then stay with me," he answered. "Stay with me forever."

"I can't," I said. "Not now. Not yet."

"Then go," he said. "Please just go."

What had I just done?

I started to walk towards the door and he said, "I will love you forever, Patrick."

I turned to face him.

"But, please don't call me anymore" he said. "I cannot go through this again."

I walked slowly out the door and out of his life thinking, *'What is wrong with me?'*

The man I'd so loved and adored just asked me to spend my life with him, and I walked out the door.

I felt alone and empty.

I honored Marty's wishes and didn't contact him again. I saw him only once after that, in Boystown, but didn't dare approach him. I couldn't bear to hurt him again.

I've never forgotten Marty, but we've lost contact. When I went back to his condo to try and reach him, he'd moved. I tried searching for him on the Internet, but had no luck.

Marty was the first man who loved me the way I wanted to be loved, the way I needed to be loved. The way anyone, man or woman, deserves to be loved. And I had just walked out of his life. I let him go.

And I had no idea if I would ever find love again.

Chapter 10 (2004)
Life after Marty

After things ended with Marty, I decided not to get involved with anyone for a while. It was just too painful walking away from someone that I loved so much. In my heart, I believed Marty had been 'the one,' and that things had gone so badly in the end was devastating for me.

Imagine hoping for one thing your entire life, finding it, and then shouting, '*No!*'

Maybe it would've been better to never have had it at all, never experienced such devotion, never known such passion, than simply to have thrown it all away as I did.

Was I cursed? Was love just something at which I was destined to fail? Had my childhood trauma ruined all chances at happiness for me? Would I ever actually heal from that terrible day?

I was sick of it all, burned out. Imagine burning out on life's most wonderful gift, the gift of love. Unbelievable. But, there I was.

I began devoting my energy to my career. I needed something to take my mind off Marty. I set goals for myself, milestones I could set to bring focus back into my life. This was important since so much of my time had been devoted to my relationship.

Instead of being a 'rebound lover,' I would work on myself for once.

I set a timeframe for purchasing my own home, and began to put away as much money as I could to accomplish this goal. I became more involved in Cynthia's after- school activities. I spent more time with my family. Every once in a while, I would go out and meet up with my friends.

I also decided to become more familiar with Chicago's gay community. If ever I was to live life as I was truly meant to, I would need to spend more time around individuals who had already come to terms with their own struggles for identity.

Before this point, I had never really connected with Halsted Street and all the interesting people from its thriving bar and club scene. When I was with Marty, we never really spent much time at these neighborhood hangouts.

One beautiful Sunday afternoon in the spring, I walked into Roscoe's. The bar was packed with gay softball players that day. I was wearing a t-shirt, shorts and a baseball cap, so I fit right in with the crowd.

Perched at the bar, I listened as these players across from me talked about the game they'd lost that day. It was pleasantly distracting, but then I heard a voice that sounded very familiar. I sat there trying to place that voice for a while, but couldn't quite figure it out. Whoever it was, he was buried in the group somewhere and I couldn't pick him out.

I stood up to get a better vantage point, pretending to look out the window, and got a good look at him. But, I still couldn't figure out how I knew him. It began to drive me a little crazy, like when a particular song gets stuck in your head and you can't remember the singer.

Then another group of players came in and the crowd got larger. The guys seated across from me made room and moved towards my side of the bar.

Then the guy with the familiar voice took off his baseball cap, and I knew.

Mike Perez grew up in my neighborhood. His older brother Ricky and I were good friends in high school. Mike was a few years younger than me, but I remembered him well. He was half Italian, half Puerto Rican, and all *punk*.

I was hesitant to say anything at first because I would be outing myself. I was, after all, sitting in a gay bar in a gay neighborhood. If Mike told his brother, then everyone from the neighborhood, my family included, would find out I was gay.

How could such a simple gesture hold such sway over my

actions? Why couldn't I just say 'hello' to an old friend? Why did things have to be so complicated?

This is why people just need to be themselves. When you have nothing to hide, life becomes so much better. But sometimes, just getting to that point can be a pretty rough road to navigate.

I sat at the bar for a couple of minutes wondering what to do. Do I go over and introduce myself, or simply walk out? What if Mike saw me leaving? Suddenly, I just decided to go for it. If saying hello to a kid from the old neighborhood, someone I hadn't seen in a long time, was somehow doing something wrong, then that was a pretty sad way to live. Anybody in that situation would probably say something, so why couldn't I?

The answer was, of course I could.

I got up and walked over to the large group of guys and looked at Mike.

"You lost, huh?" I said. "That sucks."

"Who the hell are you?" he demanded in a tough-guy voice. I just smiled and waited, and then his eyes widened and he laughed. "Do not tell me that's Pat Dati!" he said.

Mike stood up and bear-hugged me right off my feet. "I can't believe my big brother's buddy from high school is hanging out at Roscoe's!" Then he called over to a tall player chatting with some guys in the group and said, "Come over here, honey. I want you to meet somebody." Mike turned to me and said, "His name's Mike, too."

The tall guy walked over and held out his hand.

"Get outta here with that handshake shit, give him a hug!" Mike said. "He's from the old neighborhood!"

Tall Mike laughed and gave me a hug, and immediately I was a subject of some interest to all of Mike's friends because I was the guy from the straight world to which he once belonged.

"You gotta come with us," Mike said. "We're going down the street to Buck's. They sponsor the team."

We all walked down to Buck's and had a great time, just drinking beer and hanging out. Any friend of Mike's was a friend of the team's. I was starting to connect with Halsted Street.

At Buck's, Mike introduced me to a buddy of his named Tyrone Jackson, a handsome black man about ten years my junior. Tyrone and I instantly had a connection, not in a sexual way, but like we were meant to become best friends. He had a great sense of humor, and he's kept me laughing ever since.

Tyrone is also a very honest, no-nonsense guy who doesn't play games with people. With Tyrone, there's no holding back and no pretending. He says what's on his mind and doesn't like anyone getting in his face.

He's also a very proud, openly gay man who can really turn the boys' heads.

I found Tyrone impressive from the moment I met him.

I also found our friendship unlikely and strange, at first. I would have never imagined being friends with someone who was openly gay, because when you hide who you are, you tend to avoid people who don't. Birds of a feather, and all that.

Tyrone, on the other hand, thought it was strange that I was in my thirties and still had not come out of my self-imposed closet. Even crazier to him was that I had been married *twice* to women, and had a child.

Not being terribly familiar with the gay community, I assumed everyone was simply out to have sex, an assumption I have to laugh about now because it's such a common stereotype. I had been pretending to be straight for so long that I was actually thinking like it!

Tyrone and I started hanging out every weekend I didn't have Cynthia, and we had a lot of fun. He was like the Mayor of Boystown; *everyone* knew Tyrone. When we were together we were always laughing and enjoying the attention from all the guys. It's funny, because for years I worried about just being seen around the gay community, wondering how I would explain myself, but Tyrone and I had such a good time that I often forgot I was in a gay bar.

By June of 2004, I was able to buy my condo, and it meant the world to me. Granted, I'd owned two beautiful homes with my ex-wives, but I never felt like those were really *mine*.

This was a place I could really call home.

The unit was in an old, six-flat apartment building that had been gutted, rehabbed, and sold as condos in a northwest Chicago neighborhood called Albany Park. It wasn't Trump Palace, but this two-bedroom condo with exposed brick and a faux-fireplace was just right for Cynthia and me.

Since everything was brand new, I also splurged on all new furniture. It was the first time I'd actually lived on my own, and it felt fantastic. Everything about it felt fresh and exciting. My family was pleased that, after two chaotic divorces, I had finally regained control of my life.

Mom wasn't thrilled that I was moving out, but it wasn't far and she loved helping me get the place together. Albany Park is a very diverse part of Chicago that's home to at least five different nationalities. If you drive down Lawrence Avenue, the main boulevard in Albany Park, you'll likely see signs in Spanish, Korean, Polish, Indian, and Hebrew.

When I took Cynthia to an area park to play one day, I realized she was the only white child around. She noticed an Indian woman and girls wearing robes and scarves around their faces and asked, "Daddy, why do those women hide their faces?"

"Baby girl, they come from another part of the world and that's just how they dress in their culture," I explained.

My new place and neighborhood may not have been Lake Shore Drive with Marty, but it was mine, all mine.

The only thing missing was someone like Marty to share it with.

That summer, my upstairs neighbor, who was in the Army Reserves, was called to active duty in Afghanistan. He happened to knock on my door one evening when Tyrone was over to tell me he was looking for someone to lease his condo.

Tyrone asked to see it, and I thought, *'Lord, what am I in for now?'*

A month later Tyrone was the man upstairs, my very own gay guardian angel!

I must say, that was truly one of the best summers of my life. We had cookouts every other weekend with a bunch of Tyrone's friends, who quickly became my friends. We had people out on our decks calling back and forth and running up and down the stairs between our units, driving the neighbors crazy, I'm sure.

Tyrone and I became like brothers that summer, watching out for each other and developing into lifelong friends. Tyrone always had my back.

One Friday night we were out drinking and dancing at Roscoe's. It was late in the evening, the bar was packed, and I was a little drunk, out on the floor and dancing like a fool.

A cute, young guy with dirty blonde hair kept hitting on me, and even though I wasn't paying attention, Tyrone was. When my dirty blonde got a little aggressive and moved in for a kiss, Tyrone slid in between us to set things straight. A few words later, my young Casanova was in full retreat and our friends were all chanting Tyrone's name.

My hero!

That summer I met so many new friends my address book was

ready to explode. I had never felt so free. And I found it reassuring that Cynthia had now been exposed to my new life as a gay man and seemed to accept me for who I was.

She absolutely loved hanging out with 'Uncle' Tyrone. He'd come over on the weekends I had Cynthia and the three of us would watch those teen girl movies and laugh until we cried.

I still kept my gay life separate from my family and my career, but it was wonderful that I could be myself around friends like Tyrone and allow him to be a part of my daughter's life. When you love two people, you naturally want them to care for each other, too.

In some ways, I was still fooling myself, though. I really believed that no one outside of the gay community needed to know about my lifestyle other than my gay friends. Of course, that kind of belief system would never last.

But in my quest to be true to myself and live the best life possible, I was definitely moving in the right direction.

Chapter 11 (2005)
Alberto

This period was an extremely important time in my life. I was exploring gay life for the first time, and I loved it. Even though I had yet to come out to my family, I was clearly moving towards that goal, whether I realized it or not. I had gay friends and dated only men, which felt completely natural.

I was coming into my own.

Having my own place changed everything. If I had a date or wanted to bring a guy home, I didn't have to worry about someone finding out.

But even though I was dating, I wasn't really interested in a serious relationship at this point. The pain of my breakup with Marty was still lingering in my head, and besides, I was having too much fun as a single man.

But like all good things, the summer was coming to an end, and I was about to enter an even more important phase of my life.

Tyrone called me at work one day and asked me to meet him at SideTrack's after work for drinks.

"Sure," I said. "But I might get there before you because I'm only working a half day today."

"I don't care when you arrive, just look cute when you do!" he suggested.

Tyrone always knew how to make me smile.

I walked in around seven and the bar was already crowded. Everyone could feel the end of summer closing in and wanted to make the most of it.

I was wearing one of my hottest outfits: tight blue jeans and a sleeveless, blue t-shirt with metal studs running across my shoulders and down the front in the outline of a crucifix. Add cowboy boots and the Prada cologne Tyrone had given me as a gift, and I had no doubt I'd meet Tyrone's seal of approval.

SideTrack always drew the hottest guys on Friday nights, and this night was no exception. I walked through the various club rooms, scouting for Tyrone. The place was hopping, but I wasn't worried because Tyrone would always text me if he couldn't find me. I was just reveling in the buzz of club life.

As I was rounding a corner upstairs, I bumped into a tall, sultry brunette with gorgeous olive skin. He was wearing dark pants and a bright orange dress shirt that really set off his smooth, dark skin. He was strikingly handsome. Definitely someone worth the double-take.

"Excuse me," I said, and started to walk away.

"Where *you* off to so quickly?" he inquired.

I was caught off guard by his question and answered, "I'm just looking for a friend."

"I am, too," he said, and held out his hand. "I'm Alberto."

Although I found him very attractive, I just felt like hanging out with Tyrone for some mindless, end-of-summer fun. But, I shook hands and introduced myself, and when he asked if he could buy me a drink, I very nearly said 'no.'

As a matter of fact, I could feel the words forming on my lips. I had successfully avoided getting involved with anyone all summer long because I had still really not gotten over Marty. But then it hit me.

It's just one drink. What's the harm in that?

We walked over to the bar and he ordered a couple of martinis.

As we were chatting at the bar, in walks Tyrone with this little Asian guy. I waved them over and Tyrone's friend walks right up to Alberto and gives him a big hug, laughing like they were old friends.

I didn't know what was going on, but then Alberto turned to me and said, "This is my best friend, Chin!"

Tyrone laughed. "Chin and I have been friends for years, but he's been lying low lately," he said. "We ran into each other at Roscoe's."

All at once, things were starting to get more interesting.

We all hung out the rest of the night, and whenever Alberto and I talked, I really felt a connection. Alberto was a software developer for a big company based in Atlanta, but his customers were mostly located in the Midwest, so he came into town twice a month and stayed at the W Hotel on Lake Shore Drive. He owned a home in Miami, and had just ended a serious relationship.

We exchanged numbers and he promised to call the next time he was in Chicago and take me to dinner. He was a fun guy, but I figured it had already been a lovely night, and if he called, he called. I didn't have any great expectations.

Tyrone was much more excited than I was about my rendezvous with Alberto. "Chin told me Alberto thought you were cute!" he said.

I just laughed. It sounded like we were back in high school. "Maybe he'll pass me a note in study hall," I joked.

"I'm serious," Tyrone said. "I've known Chin for years, and if he vouches for someone, they're gold." He leaned in. "He's very successful, and he's looking."

Tyrone was like my very own Jewish mother.

"He just got out of a bad relationship," I said, not sure why I was being so resistant. Maybe I was just scared things wouldn't work out again if I gave my heart to someone new.

Tyrone laughed. "*Hello!*" he said. "So did you!"

True. I thought about it for a moment. "Well, I'm not calling him," I said. "He'll have to call me."

Tyrone laughed again. "You're such a heartbreaker, Patrick!"

The following Monday, I got a phone call from Alberto. He was coming to town the weekend after next and wanted to have dinner with me.

We met at Gibson's on Friday night. The place was packed, but Alberto got us a table right away. He even had a bottle of wine chilling in a bucket and appetizers waiting.

Alberto looked incredible in a white Perry Ellis button-down and Marc Jacobs slacks. We talked for hours, laughing and chatting about our respective friendships with Chin and Tyrone.

After dinner we walked down Michigan Avenue towards the lake. I knew what he was up to, but played dumb. It had been a while since I'd been on a date with a guy my age.

We walked right up to the W Hotel, of course.

"This is my hotel," he grinned. "Would you like to join me for a drink?"

"Did you have this planned?" I asked.

"Yes," he said, "but if you aren't interested, I can get you a cab."

We laughed and entered the lobby bar of the hotel and got seats overlooking the lakefront. I had not enjoyed myself romantically with anyone like this since Marty. The bar was playing Frank Sinatra tunes, which only added to the romance.

I decided this time I was going to be bold and upfront about my life story, with no surprises. I told Alberto that, while I lived as a straight man my entire life, over the past year I had met friends in the gay community and was now exploring life as a gay man. I also told him that, despite all this, I was still not out at work or to my family. Lastly, I told him about my two marriages and about my daughter, Cynthia.

None of this surprised Alberto. He thought it was fantastic that I had lived such a full life and also experienced straight life, as well. Most gay men discover and act on their sexuality at a much younger age and never really know what straight life is like.

Alberto told me he had been in a nine-year relationship that ended a few months ago, and that his ex was giving him a hard time about splitting up everything they owned. Being away from Miami and his ex was the best thing for him right now, he explained.

We talked for hours, and before we knew it, the bar was closing. But it was clear Alberto didn't want our evening to end.

"Would you come up to my suite and stay the night?" he asked. "I just want to wake up next to you tomorrow."

I agreed to spend the night with him. I'm not sure what I was thinking or if I'd had too much to drink, but I knew I was very attracted to this guy and wanted to find out more about him. This was certainly one way to do that.

A half hour later we were making out passionately on the couch in his suite, and we quickly moved to the bedroom. We practically tore each other's clothes off and jumped under the covers. After the initial awkwardness, Alberto was kissing every part of my body and we were passionately making love.

I woke up the next day in Alberto's arms, and because he was very tall - about 6'5"- and I much shorter, it all felt very safe and secure.

But that didn't mean I was totally at ease.

I didn't want to wake Alberto up, but I really wanted to leave. I'm not sure why I was in such a hurry, really. I lived alone now and had no one waiting at home to interrogate me on my whereabouts.

I managed to slip out of his arms without waking him, grabbed my things, and hurried into the bathroom. I washed up, got dressed and then started to tiptoe out of the bathroom, when he finally woke up.

"Where are you going, my little Italian Stallion?" he said.

"I didn't want to wake you," I said, awkwardly.

"Come over here, please," he gestured.

I walked over, and Alberto grabbed me and pulled me back into bed, where we again proceeded to work up a mutual appetite.

Afterwards, Alberto ordered room service. Then, he took me down to the hotel spa, where we had a massage, manicure and pedicure. Our date had turned into quite the epicurean quest.

But by this time, it was three in the afternoon, and I really did need to get home.

"As long as you're back here by eight," Alberto said, smiling.

Apparently, he'd been on the phone with Tyrone and Chin while I was in the spa, and the plan was for dinner and dancing.

Alberto certainly knew what he wanted, and he was definitely making up for lost time. I allowed myself to be swept up in his desires.

That night, the four of us went to the Chicago Chop House for dinner and polished off two bottles of Dom Pérignon with our excellent meal. After that, we all went to Roscoe's and danced until three in the morning. Another exhilarating night on the town!

For the second morning in a row, I woke up in Alberto's arms. Once more I managed to slip from his grasp without waking him, but this time I found Tyrone and Chin passed out on the sofa.

I have to say that this was a spectacular weekend. Alberto was a lot of fun and so full of life.

On Monday a dozen long stemmed roses were delivered to me at work. The card read, *'Patrick, you make me happy. I'm glad to be in your life. Love, Alberto.'*

I had never gotten flowers, or for that matter *any* gift delivered to me at work before. I walked back to my office from reception feeling very awkward. My co-workers were impressed and curious, to say the least.

"Who sent you the flowers?" one asked.

I pocketed the card. "Apparently I've got a secret admirer," I lied, hoping that would satisfy their curiosity.

This was just another reminder that I continued to live a lie. I had been exploring gay life and having a wonderful time, but I was still afraid to be out in the open, to be me. Alberto was a fantastic guy. I should have been on the top of our company roof shouting his name. But, I held back because I was afraid of being judged by my co-workers.

Fear had always impacted my life in so many ways, ever since I was a boy.

After I'd lost Marty, due to my fear of living openly as a gay man, you'd think I would have learned that self-denial lead only to unhappiness and alienation. Apparently, I still had more to learn.

Alberto started coming to Chicago more often. He still booked his suite at the *W*, but because I was getting up so early for work, he wanted to stay with me at my condo. I didn't mind; it was nice having him there. He did the nicest things while I was at work.

One morning at breakfast, he casually reminded me that I'd talked about having my place repainted.

"Someday," I said.

"What colors were you thinking about?" he inquired.

"I have no idea," I answered. "I'm no good at that stuff."

When I came home from work that day, Alberto had paint samples spread out on the coffee table for comparison. We picked out some nice colors, but I made it clear that this project would have to wait until I could afford it.

The next day when I returned home from work, my entire condo had been repainted, and it was absolutely gorgeous.

I was stunned.

"Alberto, you should not have done this," I said.

"Listen, Sweetie, he said. "I'm here all the time and *you* are paying the bills. The least I could do is help out a little."

A little? What did I do to deserve this man?

After I screwed up with Marty, I thought for a long time that I had missed my chance at happiness, but Alberto was like a second chance. He had a heart of gold and a kind, gentle soul. Surely, I wouldn't fail this time around, would I?

One weekend when I had Cynthia, Alberto asked if he could meet her. We'd been dating a few months, and if we were going to be together, the two of them would eventually be part of each other's lives, so I brought her down to the *W*.

We walked over to Navy Pier and let Cynthia pick out clothes for her doll at the American Girl Doll Store. Then, Alberto took us to lunch at the Drake Hotel on Michigan Avenue.

It was a good decision to finally get the two of them together. Cynthia adored Alberto, and when he was around her, he was like a little kid himself. He chased her around the room and got down on the floor and played and just treated her really special.

Alberto asked to meet the rest of my family, but I told him I wasn't ready for that. I had told him all about Marty and that I was just not at that point, yet. Alberto seemed to understand and didn't press the issue any further. He was just happy that I had let Cynthia be a part of our relationship.

I agonized over this, however. I couldn't help thinking that my family would likely disown me if they found out I was gay, and that would be devastating for me. I didn't honestly know if that would be their reaction, but even the thought of disappointing them would be a terrible blow. I just could not bring shame upon my family, I felt.

I still had not learned that living life in complete and total honesty is never shameful. Challenging, perhaps. But never shameful.

After dating for a few months, Alberto asked me to come out to San Francisco to meet his family. He had told them all about me, even the fact that I'd lived as a straight man most of my life and had a child. I wasn't scared to meet his family because Alberto had been openly gay all his life. I did wonder, though, if they might judge me because I had lived my life dishonestly, like a charade.

There wasn't much I could do about it, though. They would think what they wanted to think. If they accepted Alberto, I figured they would accept me, too.

It's too bad I wasn't at that point with my own family.

Alberto booked a weeklong trip in Northern California, flying us out first class. He wanted to spend a few days in San Francisco and then some time in Napa Valley before ending the trip at his sister's home in the Silicon Valley.

When we landed in San Francisco, he was almost childlike in his excitement to show me the city where he grew up. He hired a limo to take us to the *W*, and once we got settled in, he took me over to Nordstrom.

Craig, Alberto's friend from high school, ran the men's department at this Nordstrom. Alberto liked to buy his suits there so Craig could get the commission. He also wanted me to meet Craig.

Well, you would've thought Craig and Alberto were two, giggly young schoolgirls. They were so happy to see each other, and

Alberto's happiness was intoxicating. I couldn't help but take it all in.

Alberto wanted me to let Craig's assistant show me around and maybe pick out a few things for myself while he looked at some suits with Craig. But, I couldn't afford a pair of socks in that store and told him as much.

"Let Ronald show you the new fall line," Alberto said. "It's his job, and he enjoys it." So, I humored Alberto and toured the men's department with Ronald.

Ronald was a young, flamboyant guy who couldn't have been more than twenty-one years old. He was small and slender, with stylish hair and an infectious, high-pitched laugh. I liked him right away.

Alberto was right: Ronald really enjoyed his work. He had a blast having me try on different outfits over the next hour or so.

"When you come out of that dressing room, show me that you *own* those clothes," he'd say. "Walk the walk, Mr. Patrick."

When Ronald approved, he'd compliment me and put the outfit to the side; when he didn't approve, he'd let me know that, too.

During my marriages to Wendy and Jennifer, I hated shopping because neither of them allowed me to pick out clothes I actually wanted to wear. They'd always select my clothing and it was never my taste. But with Ronald, I had a great time playing dress up. We carried on like this for about two and a half hours.

Finally, Alberto had picked out about four suits and a bunch of shirts and ties, and he was ready to check out. When we got to the register, he exchanged a look with Craig, who signaled Ronald, who brought over all the clothes we'd picked out.

"Honey, it was fun shopping with Ronald, but I can't afford those items," I said.

"I'm buying them for you, Patrick," Alberto said.

"Alberto, you don't have to do that," I said. "You already brought me on this expensive trip."

He grabbed my hand and turned me around, facing the other shoppers. "Can I have your attention, please?" he announced.

Three women who looked like rich housewives shopping for their wealthy husbands gathered around. "Ladies, can I ask you a question?" said Alberto.

The women giggled and nodded.

"Do you think this man is handsome?" he asked.

I was turning three shades of red and wanted to crawl under

the clothing rack, but the women all thought he was darling and agreed that I was just as Alberto had described.

"And sexy, too!" Craig chimed in.

"Well, I'm proud to tell you, he's my boyfriend," Alberto continued, as the women smiled and encouraged him. "Is there anything wrong with me treating him special and buying him nice things?" he asked.

Needless to say, the women were in full agreement, and we walked out of the store with our arms filled with bags and boxes.

It felt fabulous to be treated with such love and respect, something I'd never felt with Wendy or Jennifer. Who in their right mind would not want to be treated as Alberto treated me? Mind you, I was still pretty embarrassed about that little presentation in the department store. This man was telling total strangers that he loved me and wanted to take care of me. I loved the attention that day, but it was also awkward because Alberto made me feel more openly gay than ever before.

I felt out of my element. There was love and chemistry, but I still wasn't sure I could ever totally embrace life as a gay man.

The next morning we explored the city. I bought Cynthia an Oriental dress in Chinatown, and we took a cable car to Fisherman's Wharf. We drove over the Golden Gate Bridge, of course. We were like kids on a playground, having the time of our lives.

Alberto was very romantic and would kiss me in each local spot we visited. He would ask other tourists to take silly pictures of us in every location. I honestly had never acted like that before. I think that after my rape in childhood I lost what it felt like to be a kid. I was consumed with guilt, even though none of it was my fault, and that was a terrible burden to shoulder decade in and out. I lost a lot of my youth that day. I had found moments of happiness, but I was too sad, too often.

I think back on all the times my mom would ask why I was so unhappy. I wanted to tell her that the bad man hurt me and beat me and raped me, but I knew it would shock and hurt her to hear that kind of admission.

Alberto and I spent the next few days touring wineries in Napa Valley. The vineyards were beautiful and the wine was amazing. The fields, brimming with luscious green and purple grapes, were breathtaking. We stayed at an adorable bed and breakfast, watched the sun set from the deck every evening, and held hands as we talked about our lives. It was not all about sex, and that was what I really appreciated about Alberto. He brought out the kid in me, and restored some of what had been stolen from me so many years ago.

Alberto made me happy.

We ended the trip at his sister's house. I was nervous to meet his family because I was uncertain how they'd receive me. There was no good reason for this particular feeling, but it persisted nonetheless.

As we drove up to his sister's house, two adorable little girls with long black ponytails and matching dresses came rushing out, screaming excitedly for their playful uncle. They were followed by Alberto's sister and her husband.

They all hugged Alberto, and then his sister turned to me and said, "You must be Patrick."

"Yes," I said shyly.

"Get over here and give me a big hug" she said. "My brother has been talking about you for months, now!"

She grabbed me and whispered, "You're even cuter than he said."

I was blushing like a child when she finally let go of me, and when I reached out to shake her husband's hand, he just said, "In this family, we give hugs," and he pulled me in, too.

I was overwhelmed by how gracious and loving they all were. With Alberto's family, there was no pretending. They loved each other without reservation or qualification. It really made me wonder if my family could ever be that way with my partner.

Providing, that is, they were able to accept *me*.

It also made me think about the differences between Marty and Alberto. Marty never got along with his parents, and Alberto had a loving, accepting family. I envied the relationship he shared with his family and how everyone was so accepting. Alberto's family loved him for who he was and what he was: a son, a brother, an uncle, and a friend.

Even more touching to me was seeing Alberto's mother tear up when she saw him. We had a wonderful visit and I got to see another side of Alberto that I had not seen before. I was truly falling in love with this man. Everything about him was amazing and real.

After returning from our trip, Alberto told me he wanted to move to Chicago. He didn't want to be on a plane all the time, which I could understand. And instead of staying at the *W*, he started staying with me. At first I didn't mind, but gradually it started to interfere with time to myself.

I had never had alone time until that year, and it had become very important to me. For the first time in my life, I had my own place and didn't have to answer to anyone. When I was married to Jennifer, she demanded I be home at six o'clock every day. When I lived with my parents, even as a grown man, I had to be accountable for when I was not at home with them.

Being in my own place gave me freedom I have never known before, and that was hard to give up.

*****

One Sunday, Alberto, Tyrone, Chin and I all went to watch a football game at a sports bar in Lincoln Park. This meant venturing outside our familiar gay community and entering into 'straight bar' territory. Two attractive girls were working as models promoting Miller Lite Beer. They were giving out free promotional items and flirting with most of the guys in the bar.

When they got to our table they stopped to talk to us, and didn't realize at first that we were gay. After a while they figured Tyrone and Chin were, but they didn't care, they were just having fun with us.

After some time had passed and we were thinking of leaving to return back to our side of town, Tyrone suggested the girls go out with us back in Boystown.

"Are all you guys gay?" one of them asked.

"Yeah," Tyrone said, and then pointed to Alberto and me. "These two are a couple."

They both looked at me in my football jersey and said, "We would have never guessed *you* were gay."

All of a sudden I felt labeled, defined by my sexuality, and it made me very uncomfortable. I was being judged by straight people for being gay. It didn't feel right to me. I didn't appreciate the fact that these two girls were identifying me as homosexual.

When Alberto and I got back to my place, he could sense that something was bothering me, but I couldn't talk about it. I barely slept that night.

Why did what those girls thought bother me so much?

I realized later it was because that was the first time I had been called out on who I really was, a gay man.

The next day, Alberto left on business and would be gone until the following weekend. I had a lot to think about in his absence.

The following weekend Cynthia had a soccer game in the

suburbs. Alberto flew back into town on Friday, and I woke up the next day to go watch Cynthia's game. Since Alberto had been staying with me while he was in town, he wanted to do something special and bought new drapes for my living room.

That evening when I returned home from Cynthia's soccer game, I looked at what Alberto had done with my place. It was wonderful. He later wanted to take me to dinner so we could spend time alone. Alberto knew something was bothering me, but we just let the night go on without mentioning it.

We met up with Tyrone and Chin to hang out and then went over to the *W* to spend the night. Alberto kept asking me what was wrong and all I could think of was those two, young girls from the straight bar calling me out. I wanted to tell him how I felt, but I didn't think he would understand. I had been living as a straight man my whole life, and now I was gay in my thirties. My strict upbringing and Catholic faith only made matters more intractable. Maybe it was the fear that my family would disown me or that I would humiliate them, but I was still unable to fully realize the person I wanted to be at this point.

Alberto flew out on Monday and called as soon as he landed. He wanted to know what was wrong, whether he'd done something to make me unhappy.

"I just need some space," I said.

The next day he flew back unexpectedly and told me to meet him at the condo. I was at work when he called but told him I would leave to meet him.

When I got to my place Alberto was sitting on the front stairs. He looked sad and upset. When he saw me, he started to cry. Suddenly, I felt like I was watching a movie replay of Marty and me.

"I don't know what's bothering you lately," he said, "but I want you to know something."

"Alberto, please –"

"I want to spend the rest of my life with you, Patrick. I want to make you and Cynthia my family."

"Don't do this to me, Alberto," I said. "You know what happened with Marty. I can't have it happen again. Not with you."

"I don't care about you and Marty," he cried. "That's in the past. I love you and I'm ready to move my life for you."

I just stared at him -- this man I loved, this man who didn't deserve to be rejected, this man who had been nothing but wonderful to me.

"I just want you to tell me you love me and that you want to spend your life with me, too," he continued. "I want you both in my life."

"Alberto, I can't answer that question right now."

"Patrick, you're a wonderful man with a lot of love to give, but when are you going to stop giving and let others give to you?"

"It's complicated, Alberto."

"No, it's not. You just have to let yourself be happy. You let me in and you loved me and when I want to love you back, you run away. You make me so happy, Patrick. Why won't you let me do the same for you? Why won't you let me love you?"

"I just need some time, Alberto," I said, but even as the words escaped my lips, I knew they rang hollow. It was exactly what I'd said to Marty.

"You shared your secrets with me, and I know it's difficult," he said. "But I will never hurt you, Patrick. I love you with all my heart. Just let me love you."

"Why can't we just spend more time getting to know each other? I love you, Alberto, and I don't want to lose you. Please just give me more time," I pleaded.

I'd never seen a man look so defeated.

"You don't need time," he said. "You need to let someone *in*. People love you but you won't let them inside. And until you do, you'll always be alone, Patrick."

I started to cry. It was all happening again, and I felt powerless to stop it.

"Why are you so worried about what other people think?" he asked. "Why are you so afraid to be who you *are*?"

I had no answer for him.

Alberto reached out and took my hand. I felt the cool metal of my house keys against my palm, and knew our hands would never touch again after that. I followed him out to the street, crying and begging him not to go, but his mind was made up.

Just let me love you, he'd said. Why was that so hard to do?

Chapter 12 (2005 – 2008)
Bradley – Darkness and Light

One day, Tyrone suggested I join Match.com to meet some nice, single guys on-line. I wasn't really interested, but then one night Tyrone and I were playing around on the computer and we created a profile for myself and posted photos. Then we sent messages to guys we thought were cute. We were acting like silly teenagers just having a good time. Every few days I would look through the responses I received from my profile.

It felt good to have people expressing an interest in me again. I think my insecure side needed assurance that I was attractive and worthy of finding someone special. I didn't take any of it too seriously. I was just having fun and thought if I met someone we'd have a date and see what happens. After rejecting Marty and Alberto, I had kind of given up on serious relationships. I'd made a pact with myself that *were* I to fall in love again, I would finally leave my self-imposed closet once and for all and live openly as a gay man. I didn't want to lie anymore to my family and the people who loved me. But I was still afraid, and I was still hiding.

One day I got a 'match' response from a guy in California. I had received many responses from guys locally but none from other states, especially one so far away. His name was Bradley and he lived in Los Angeles. His email read: 'I saw your picture and profile and you sound and look like a very nice guy and I would like to chat with you sometime.' I reviewed his profile and pictures. He was very attractive: dark hair, green eyes, and short but with a nice build. I decided to email him back: 'You sound like a great guy but why are you responding to guys in Chicago?' He replied that he'd lived in LA for 12 years and was tired of California guys. He also mentioned that he found Midwesterners to be 'down to earth and grounded.' I felt flattered but told him that, while it was very nice of him to say all this, I had no plans to move to California anytime soon. He wrote back and asked if he could have my number and if we could talk sometime. I thought to myself, well, what is there to lose by simply talking with this guy? I wrote back, gave him my number, and told him to call me sometime.

A few days later, on a Saturday when I was at the park with Cynthia, my cell phone rang. Cynthia was playing on the slide and I was watching her. When I answered the phone, the person on the other end said, "Hello Patrick, this is Bradley from Match.com calling from California."

I was startled because I never thought he'd actually call and paused before I said anything.

He said, "Hello, are you there, Patrick?"

"Yes, I'm sorry you caught me off guard," I said.

He said, "You didn't think I'd call did you?"

I said, "Honestly, no. I thought you were just being nice asking for my phone number."

He asked what I was doing and I told him that I was at the park with my daughter. He said, "I'm sorry, I don't want to disturb you now."

I said, "It's fine, she's playing with the other children right now."

Bradley began the conversation by saying he lived in LA and worked in real estate. He mentioned that, as we were speaking, he was at an open house in a huge mansion in Hollywood.

I said, "Well, that sounds great." I really wasn't interested in where this conversation was heading and wanted to get back to Cynthia.

"Listen Bradley," I said. "Do you think we can talk another time? I have to take my daughter back home for lunch."

He said, "No problem, we can talk another time."

I said, "That sounds great." I was relieved to end the conversation, because Bradley seemed so self-centered. I didn't want to waste his time or mine.

When I thought about that call, it all seemed very strange. Why was a guy who lived thousands of miles away expressing an interest in me? I decided to just forget about him. A few days passed and, while I was at work eating lunch, I went online to check my email. As soon as I open my mail, up pops a message from Bradley. 'Wow, this guy is persistent,' I thought.

I opened the message and it read, 'Patrick, it was so nice talking to you the other day. You sound like a very masculine guy, which is just my type. I'm sorry I disturbed you while you were with your daughter. Could we set up time to talk again on the phone when you're not busy?'

Again, this all seemed very peculiar to me. Why waste our time on the phone when I knew it was not going to go anywhere? I didn't want to be rude, so I wrote back and told him that we could talk next week. I didn't specify a call-time thinking that if he wanted to call, he would.

The following Sunday I was out with Tyrone. We had decided to meet up with our friend, Rico, at a gay bar called Jack Hammer. Rico tended bar on weekends at this leather bar to make extra cash. The bar is dark and kind of sleazy, but Rico worked on the back patio in the summer so we could sit outside. The patio was great because it was surrounded with lots of plants and flowers. You could also take your shirt off and get a tan while you drank.

It was a hot August day and we were having a ball on the patio. Tyrone was making fun of some guys attempting to pick up a man sitting at the bar. We were laughing and having a great time. All of a sudden my phone rings and I don't recognize the number.

"Hello?" I said.

The person on the other end of the phone said, "Hello Patrick, it's Bradley."

I was buzzed from my beer and replied by saying, "Bradley *who*?"

He said, "This is Bradley from California. We met on Match.com"

I was still confused but said, "Yes, right."

The music on the patio was loud and Tyrone was screaming for me to come back to the bar.

Bradley said, "It sounds like you're having a good time!"

I said, "I'm with my friends drinking beer on a hot summer day in Chicago."

"Well, I am at a house-showing in Beverly Hills, and it's a nice cozy house," he laughed.

I said, "Listen Bradley, can we talk another time because I'm with my friends and they are getting a little crazy."

He said, "Sure, no problem, I'll call you next week."

"Great, sorry, gotta go," I said, and then hung up.

I walked back to Tyrone and he asked, "Who was on the phone? Cynthia?"

I said, "No, it was some strange guy I met on Match.com."

Tyrone said, "Is he cute? If he is, you should call him back and invite him to the bar."

I said, "That's not possible because he lives in California."

Tyrone said, "Why would some guy from Match.com be calling you from California?"

"He saw my profile and thinks I'm handsome," I replied.

Tyrone said, "That is just not right to me, some guy calling from California." He continued his point that this call made no sense. "If the guy lives in California, he should look for a boyfriend there," said Tyrone.

"I agree, it is strange, so let's forget about him and have fun," I said.

A few days later, I had just got home from work when my phone rang. It was Bradley again. I was really in no mood to talk with him but again did not want to be rude. That's typical me -- feeling sorry for someone I didn't know but feeling the need to please him, anyway.

Bradley said, "Is now a good time to talk?"

Reluctantly, I said, "Sure, I just got home from work."

I decided to just listen to this guy and then tell him that I wasn't interested in meeting someone from another state. He told me all about his life in LA, that he was born and raised in Canada and that, while in high school, his family relocated to Texas. After high school, he moved to New York to attend college and then, after college, he moved to California. The conversation centered entirely on him, but I was okay with that.

Then Bradley asked me what I did for a living. I said, "I work as the Director of Marketing for a major book publishing company in Chicago."

He asked me, "Do you like your work?"

I said, "Yes, it's great."

He then said, "What do you like most about it?"

I replied, "I get to travel every other month to New York and

California."

I explained that our company maintained offices in both locations and that I was responsible for managing marketing efforts in those two offices.

Bradley then asked, "What part of California is your office in?"

I told him it was in Santa Monica and he replied, "That's not far from Los Angeles at all."

I said, "Yes, I know. I sometimes fly into LAX."

After a few more minutes I said, "I'm sorry, but I have to eat dinner now."

Bradley said, "Can I call you again?

I really did not understand why he wanted to continue talking because it was obvious that I wasn't interested. But I said, "Sure."

The next Sunday Tyrone and I decided to go out for drinks at Sidetrack; on Sunday's they do show tunes. The bar draws a huge crowd of gay men on that day and everyone sings along to the music. I always enjoy watching grown men bellowing at the top of their voices as they belt out "Somewhere over the Rainbow" along with Judy Garland.

The place was packed and thriving on this particular day. Once we were in the main bar area, I saw my friend Tony leaning against the wall by himself. I had met Tony at Roscoe's several weeks ago and found him very interesting. He's Italian-American and grew up on the northwest side of the city, just as I did. Both of us attended the same high school, though he graduated years ahead of me. Tony was about ten years older than me and always in fantastic shape. He once worked as a talent scout for the Chicago White Sox and spent a good deal of time on the road trying to discover the next, great baseball hero.

Tony looks and acts a bit like the actor Joe Pesci. He's a short, stocky guy with dark black hair, and though always a stylish dresser, you'd never think of Tony as being gay. He had been married once while in his twenties and divorced only a few years later. Tony was not openly gay and could easily pass for straight. Actually, Tony will never *admit* that he's gay. He just tells people that he 'likes men.' In truth, he hasn't been with a woman since he left his ex-wife in the '80s.

I always feel comfortable around Tony because he acts very straight, and we both grew up in similar neighborhoods and families. Tony married his now ex-wife early on because that's what Italian guys from the northwest side were expected to do. It never bothered Tony to conceal the fact that he was gay. I figured it was his business and that no one needed to know the truth. I could appreciate Tony's attitude, though I also think it caused him to miss out on a lot in life, including a real lover.

I told Tyrone I was going to say hello to Tony and that I would join him on the other side of the bar in a few minutes. I walked up to Tony and said, "What's up, bud?"

Tony said, "What are you doing here, Patrick?"

I said, "I'm here with my friend, Tyrone."

Tony and I leaned on the bar and caught up on each other's lives over the next several minutes. Then Tony said, "Let me buy you a drink." Tony approached the bar and ordered two vodkas on the rocks, his favorite drink. I had to remember: when Tony buys you a drink, you drink what *he* drinks. A few minutes later a guy across the bar waves at Tony.

"Patrick, can you wait here for just a minute?" he said. "I see someone I know on the other side of the bar and just want to say hello."

I said, "Sure Tony, go ahead. I'll save our spot."

Tony walked over to the guy and, while they're talking, I notice the guy pointing in my direction and Tony smiling.

A few minutes later Tony came back and said, "The guy I was talking with works out at my gym."

I said, "That's cool."

Tony said, "He just told me that he grew up with you and that you two went to grammar school together."

I said, "Really, what's his name?"

Tony said, "His name is Jeffrey Fuller."

I said, "That's strange, I don't remember that name."

Tony then said, "Jeffrey is *not* one of your fans, Patrick."

I said, "What do you mean?"

He said, "Jeffrey said that when you were kids in sixth grade you were good friends, but when you found out he was gay you stopped being his friend." Tony also said that Jeffrey told him my friends and I made his life a living hell in grammar school.

Tony said, "Jeffrey is very angry with you, Patrick, and he's shocked to see you in a gay bar."

It all came back to me. I had forgotten Jeffrey and his impact on my life when we were kids. I felt terrible and said, "Tony, please come with me because I have to apologize to Jeffrey."

Tony said, "Patrick, that's not a good idea."

I said, "No Tony, I was mean to Jeffrey and I feel awful about my behavior."

We walked over to Jeffrey and the guy who was with him. I said, "Hello, Jeffrey. It's me, Patrick Dati."

Jeffrey replied, "I remember you."

I said, "Listen Jeffrey, that was a long time ago and kids do stupid things. I want to apologize for the way I treated you when we were kids."

He said, "Patrick, when we were kids, you teased me and treated me like a freak, and now you stand in front of me as a gay man."

I replied, "Jeffrey, you couldn't 'hide.' I could. I saw myself in you and it scared me. I don't know how to tell you – how to say how much it scared me. So, I was cruel because I was so scared of being my real self. And I hid ... because I could. I'm sorry I hurt you. I hurt you, I know. I hurt myself more, though."

Then I told him I had been married twice and have a daughter.

Jeffrey said, "Did you know I still live on the next block over from your parents?"

I said, "No, I thought you moved away."

Jeffrey told me his parents had passed away years earlier and had left their home to him. Then, he introduced me to his boyfriend, Anthony, who he had been with for the past 12 years. I bought them both drinks and we spent the next hour catching up with each other. By the end of the evening, Jeffrey and I were friends again, and we exchanged phone numbers and promised to get together for dinner in the future.

The following week, Bradley contacted me again and our conversations started to get more appealing. He started to open up about his family, and I got to know more about him. During one conversation, Bradley told me he wanted to come to Chicago for a visit. He told me his best female friend from high school lived in Chicago and that he'd promised her he would come visit. Then, Bradley said he wanted to meet me.

He said, "If we're not attracted to each other, then I'll just go stay with my friend for a couple days."

I thought this was all moving too fast, but agreed anyway - if it didn't work I would not feel obligated to continue anything. Or, so I thought at the time. I agreed to pick up Bradley at O'Hare when he flew into town.

Bradley arrived on a Friday afternoon and planned to stay through Sunday. I pulled up at the United Airlines terminal to meet him outside the baggage area. I sat waiting in my white

Chevy Camaro, anxious to see what this guy looked like in person. I had described my car so Bradley would find me easily. Within a few minutes there was a tap on the passenger window and this handsome guy standing outside the door with a warm smile on his face. I got out of the car and reached out to shake his hand, but Bradley took my hand and pulled me towards him for a kiss. I accepted the kiss, grabbed his bag and tossed it in the trunk.

When we got into my car Bradley said, "I *figured* you'd be driving a sports car." Then he said, "I see you have a rosary hanging from your mirror. Can I assume you're Catholic?"

I replied, "Yes, I am Roman Catholic and attend mass every week." Bradley said he was Jewish but did not practice. He also mentioned that he had attended Catholic masses in the past and really enjoyed the experience.

We were already attracted to each other. Bradley was wearing a pair of shorts, a t-shirt and tennis shoes. He had black, short-cropped hair and green eyes. Bradley was my height with a nice build; I could tell he worked out. I was wearing tight jeans, a t-shirt and my cowboy boots. Bradley told me I looked more handsome in-person than in my pictures. The feeling was mutual, I told him.

When we approached my city block and stopped in front of my condo I said, "Well, this is where I live." We parked, I grabbed his bag and Bradley followed me into my building. After opening the door to my place, I showed him in and gave him a quick tour of the place. Bradley told me he liked what he saw. He then asked if he could use my bathroom. "Sure," I said, and then asked, "Hey, can I grab you a beer?" Bradley replied, "Sure, I'd like that."

After emerging from the bathroom, Bradley joined me in the living room. He walked over to the fireplace and looked at all the pictures on the mantel of Cynthia and me. He told me, "Your daughter is very beautiful, and I can tell you are very proud of her."

I replied, "Yes, Cynthia is the love of my life."

Bradley asked how long it had been since my divorce from Wendy. I told him that we separated when Cynthia was one year old and the divorce was then finalized when she was three - over six years, now. He then asked, "Do they know you're gay?"

I said, "No, not yet. Cynthia is only nine years-old now, and I want to wait until she's mature enough to really understand."

I told Bradley that I bring Cynthia to the gay neighborhood to shop and that she has met several of my friends who are gay. But at this point in her life, I explained, it wasn't important to explain my sexuality to her.

I handed Bradley a beer and turned on the radio. As we sat on the sofa listening to music, Bradley moved closer to me and asked if he could kiss me. I told him, "Sure" and we had our first real kiss. It was a very passionate kiss and lasted several minutes. Then Bradley said, "I have been waiting to do that for a long time." I smiled and, moments later, he started taking off my clothes.

He then said, "Can we lie in your bed?" I said, "Sure" and he followed me into the bedroom. We made out for a while and then Bradley whispered in my ear, "I want you to make love to me." I started to run my hands over his body. He had very little body hair, though. Bradley started to rub my chest and told me he liked the hair on my body.

He then turned over and said, "Make love to me like you've never made love to anyone before." We proceeded to have sex and though it was very enjoyable, Bradley just lay there with very little reaction. I also noticed he never got an erection. I didn't think much of it, though. I just thought this guy is a 'bottom' and that was that.

After we were done having sex, I asked Bradley if he wanted to take a shower with me and he said yes. When we were showering, I commented on his smooth body and Bradley told me he had all his body hair cosmetically removed. He told me it cost him a lot of time, money, and pain but that he liked it this way. Bradley told me everyone in Los Angeles has it done.

That evening I took Bradley to Andersonville, a mostly gay neighborhood on the north side, where we dined at a popular Italian restaurant called Angelina's. We shared a bottle of red wine, and the night was all very romantic. After dinner we went to Fritz's martini bar for their signature cocktails. We looked like the perfect gay couple because we were both about the same height and body-type.

Bradley had a very strong personality. He expressed himself openly and did not give much thought to what he was saying. When we were drinking at Fritz's, a young straight couple was sitting next to us at the bar. Now, Fritz's is a small cozy bar with stylish, modern decor. The bartenders wear white dress shirts with black bow ties. It's an upscale bar that attracts business professionals, mostly gay. On Friday nights, though, the bar is packed with a mix of both gay and straight customers.

The cute straight couple seated next to us appeared to have just recently met. Bradley leaned over and said to the young woman, "Are you two on a date?"

The young lady said, "Yes, and how about you?"

Bradley replied, "Yes, I just flew in today from LA to meet this guy. My name is Bradley and this is my boyfriend, Patrick."

I felt a bit uneasy because I had just met this guy today and he had just introduced me to strangers as his 'boyfriend.' I smiled awkwardly, shook the couple's hands and then said, "Hello." Bradley then proceeded to tell the couple that we had met on Match.com, and that we'd been corresponding online and by phone for months. He also told them he was so happy he'd met a guy from the Midwest, because he hated the guys in LA.

I was not sure what to think about this conversation. I felt uncomfortable because this was only our first date. Throughout the night, Bradley continued to introduce me to people as his boyfriend. I found this behavior very odd, but just figured maybe this was common practice in LA and that Bradley just wanted to let everyone know he was 'taken.' We later went back to my place and made our way to the bedroom. Bradley again asked me to make love to him. Of course I wanted to because he was sexy and good-looking, but I also thought the evening was odd and unsettling.

The next day, Bradley had planned to visit his high school friend, Beth, who lived in Lincoln Park. Lincoln Park is an upscale neighborhood just north of downtown Chicago, populated mostly by professionals. Bradley said Beth was a woman who had "done well for herself." What he *meant* was that she had married a wealthy, older man to take care of her. The couple had three young daughters. Bradley also revealed that Beth had undergone a lot of cosmetic surgery and looked nothing like she did in high school.

When Bradley and I drove up Beth's street, I noticed that all the homes were huge and their owners obviously rich. We pulled into Beth's driveway and pressed the bell on the house gate. A young woman with a foreign accent answered and said, "Can I help you?"

I responded saying, "We're here to visit Mrs. Walton."

The woman said, "Can I ask who you are?"

I replied, "Patrick and Bradley."

She said, "When the gate opens, pull up to the garage. Mrs. and Mr. Walton are waiting for you on the patio."

Bradley said, "I am so excited to see Beth and Walter. It's been years since we saw each other at our high school reunion."

Beth and Walter's home was picture-perfect, something right out of *Better Homes and Gardens*. Bradley and I were both dressed for the hot summer day in casual t-shirts and shorts. We didn't really look like we belonged in this neighborhood, let alone guests visiting this lavish home.

Beth and Walter were sitting on a beautiful patio which was filled with lush flowers and perfectly manicured hedges and shrubs. They were a good looking couple. Beth was blonde and had a great body, a 39 year-old woman who had birthed three children yet looked like a supermodel. Walter was in his late fifties, tall with dark hair and graying temples, and still very handsome. This was Beth's first marriage and Walter's second. It was obvious to me that Beth was a trophy wife and very proud of it. Walter made his fortune in the costume jewelry business. He manufactured the jewelry in Japan and sold it to discount department stores in the United States.

Now, I knew Bradley was from LA and somewhat pretentious, but from the moment we set foot onto Beth's patio, he became a totally different person. All at once, Bradley appeared extremely pretentious and shallow. He spent most of the afternoon showering Beth with ingratiating compliments about her physical appearance and her amazing life. He told Beth she was the most beautiful woman in Chicago and that they needed to go shopping together the next time he came to town.

Bradley had studied fashion design at college in New York and his goal was to be a personal shopper for rich women. He had always dreamt of owning a business as a personal shopper for wealthy woman needing his assistance to look their very best. It didn't seem to be a practical way of making a living to me, though.

Beth gave us a tour of their home, which reminded me of the life I lived with Jennifer. The home was huge and luxurious and had amenities that just did not seem practical to me. Then again, it was their money and they could spend it how they wanted, I figured. We had lunch with Beth and Walter on the patio and at one point their children came out and were introduced. They seemed like programmed robots on automatic. They were nice kids but unreal to me.

At one point Bradley asked Beth if he could see her wardrobe, to get a look at the latest fashions. Beth thought this would be fun. She looked at Walter and said, "Do you mind, honey?" Walter said, "Go ahead, sweetie, have fun. I'll stay here and entertain Patrick."

I was uncomfortable with this idea because Walter and I had nothing in common except that I was once married to a woman as rich as him. Walter asked if I would join him in their library for some bourbon. I followed him into the house, and we entered this beautiful room with cherry-wood walls and a huge moose head hanging over the fireplace. Behind a wall he had opened was a liquor cabinet full of expensive booze.

Walter asked me, "What type of bourbon would you like, Patrick?" I didn't even like bourbon, so I said, "I'll have whatever you're having, Walter."

Walter poured us our drinks and then sat with me in front of a huge fireplace. He told me that he'd met Bradley a few times when he and Beth attended her high school reunions. Walter admitted he didn't know much about Bradley other than his passion for hanging out with Beth and helping her pick out expensive clothing.

Walter said that Beth had mentioned Bradley's excitement over meeting me and how much he hoped things would work out between us. I said, "Honestly Walter, Bradley and I just met online about a month ago. He seems like a nice guy, but this is only the second day we've been together."

Walter replied, "Is that a fact? Beth told me that Bradley thinks the world of you and really wants things to work out. Bradley is looking to move to Chicago soon to start a new life."

I looked at Walter and said, "He didn't tell *me* that."

Walter said, "I apologize. Maybe I wasn't supposed to say anything. Forget I even said that." After a moment, he said, "Maybe Bradley is just thinking this relationship will give him new hope for a fresh start in life."

A short while later, Beth and Bradley joined us in the library. Walter and Beth had plans to attend the opera that evening, so Bradley and I needed to be on our way soon.

They walked us back to the patio and Bradley kissed Beth on both cheeks and said, "I am so happy I was able to visit with you both."

I shook Walter's hand and then Beth's. Beth then said, "I hope we see a lot more of you, Patrick."

Bradley then replied, "If I have anything to do about it, you will."

On the drive home Bradley asked what I thought of Beth and

Walter. I couldn't be honest with Bradley. They were both very nice and polite but to me they seemed superficial, phony. They seemed like the type of people I encountered in my life with Jennifer. Those memories were not fond ones and I did not fit in well with these kinds of people.

Bradley told me Beth thought I was cute and that the two of us made the perfect couple. Bradley was so happy that his best friend from high school approved of his new relationship. I then thought to myself: this is our first visit with each other and he thinks we're already in a relationship!

The next day I drove Bradley to the airport. When I dropped him off at his terminal he said, "Honey, I had a fantastic weekend with you. I don't want to leave you because I am going to miss you so much."

I just couldn't figure this guy out. This was all too much, too soon. I was not nearly as involved as he was, but I couldn't let on. I told him, "I had a great time too, and I'm looking forward to seeing you again."

Bradley said, "You have plans to visit your Santa Monica office soon?"

I said, "Yes, I have to be there next month."

Bradley asked if we could see each other then and I replied, "Sure, that would be nice."

Over the next few weeks Bradley called me every day. He would tell me all about his day and how much he missed me. I was confused because although I thought he was a nice guy I did not feel whatever he was obviously feeling. I didn't tell anyone about Bradley because I was not sure it would last. It seemed unlikely.

The next month I went to our Santa Monica office to work on some marketing plans. I arrived on a Wednesday and was going to return by Friday. I had phoned Bradley to tell him he was welcome to join me at my hotel. He met me on Wednesday evening and we went to dinner, and then we went back to my hotel room and had sex. The next day Bradley asked if he could stay in Santa Monica and wait for me to get done with work because he wanted to show me his home. I was fine with that idea, but I also wondered why he wasn't concerned about being at work that day.

That evening we drove back to Bradley's place because he wanted me to meet his dogs, Rusty and Peanut. They were delightful. Then, he introduced me to his neighbor, Rich. Rich was not very welcoming. He was very sarcastic, and I could tell he didn't like me. When Bradley and I went to dinner that evening, I told him how I felt about Rich's shabby treatment of me.

Bradley said, "Don't, Rich is jealous of you."

I said, "Why?"

Bradley said, "Because Rich and I were a couple at one time, but I broke up with him."

I thought this was all very strange. Not because Rich and Bradley had been a couple once, but that they currently lived in the same building and were best friends. I left California the next day not knowing what to think of Bradley. To say the least, I was ambivalent.

That next week Bradley called me every day. While I did find him attractive and the sex to be good, something just wasn't right with Bradley. One day, during one of our phone conversations, Bradley asked if I wanted to meet him in Las Vegas for a long weekend. He said he knew of a great gay hotel off the strip. I thought I could use a long weekend to relax and get away so I agreed.

The hotel was filled with men who arrived there for a gay convention for 'bears.' Bears are typically large, hairy gay men who are sexually attracted to each other. The hotel was tacky and located in a seedy, off-the-strip area of Las Vegas.

Once we checked in, Bradley and I walked to the grocery store to pick up some snacks. When we got back to the room, we put on our swimsuits and headed to the pool area. When we entered the pool area, there were large, naked, hairy gay men lying on lawn chairs around the pool. Several of them were in the pool playing water volleyball.

When Bradley and I walked to the corner of one side of the pool everyone stared at us. Well, here we were, two smaller-sized men in good shape wearing tiny, little swimsuits. I trimmed my body hair before coming to Vegas and we had both been working out to look buff for the trip. We stuck out like sore thumbs. We sat in an area where we could be by ourselves, reading our magazines and occasionally looking at some guest running around naked.

After about a half hour, the guys playing pool volleyball started purposely hitting the ball in our direction. Of course, I kept retrieving the ball and tossing it back to them. The next time this happened Bradley said, "They are doing that because they want to look at your ass, Patrick."

I said, "Bradley please, we're not their type."

Bradley said, "These guys are into *every* type, and I don't appreciate my boyfriend playing their stupid games."

I said, "Come on Bradley, they're harmless ... and I'm not interested in these guys, anyway. I'm here with you."

Bradley said, "If that's true, then when the ball comes over here again don't get up and get it for them."

I said, "Come on, it's funny."

"I don't think it's funny, Patrick," Bradley replied.

A few minutes later the ball flew over our chairs and Bradley looked at me, lowered his sun glasses and said, *"Do not move, Patrick."*

I sensed Bradley's power controlling me and I did not like it. I looked down at my magazine and continued to read. One of the hairy guys in the pool said, "Hey mister swimsuit guy, can you please get our ball again?"

I looked at them and then looked over at Bradley. Bradley got up from his chair and approached the edge of the pool. He pulled off his sunglasses and said, "My boyfriend is not here to be your ball retriever, gentlemen. We're on vacation and would prefer not to be included in your games."

I was stunned because these guys were huge and could have killed us. Then Bradley walked over to me, leaned down, grabbed my head and started making out with me. I pulled back and said, "Bradley, what are you trying to prove?"

He said, "I want these guys to know you're with me, and that you're not just another piece of meat."

I said, "Bradley, I don't like the way you're behaving."

He then hastily grabbed his stuff and stormed back to the hotel room.

Once he left, the guys in the pool said, "What's up with your boyfriend?"

I said, "Sorry guys, he's just in a bad mood."

I left the pool area because I felt like a jerk and wanted to be away from the situation. When I got back to the room Bradley was lying on the bed. I said, "Honey, what's up with you?"

He said, "If you came to fuck someone else then go back down and do everyone at the pool."

I said, "Bradley, where is this coming from?"

He said, "You don't want to be here with me. You just want to flirt with all the other men."

I said, "Please Bradley, you think I came all the way from Chicago and paid for this trip for both of us just to fool around with other guys?"

Bradley said, "If you really feel that way, then make love to me right now."

I said, "Bradley, after what just happened, I'm not exactly in the mood at the moment."

He said, "You slut. You want someone else."

I said, "No, I don't. I want you."

Then he said, "So, if you mean that, make love to me."

I took off my swim suit and got into bed with him. Bradley grabbed my head and said, "I want you to make love to me like you have never done it before."

I said, "Okay honey, that sounds good to me."

I really wasn't into it, but I wanted to please Bradley.

Then Bradley said, "Before we get started let me get something from the bathroom." After about 5 minutes, he came back, took off his swim suit, and climbed into bed. He kissed me and said, "Baby, make love to me."

I was a little intoxicated at this point and was just going with it. I got on top of Bradley and we started to make love. We were both into the love making when Bradley started to scream, "Do it to me, baby, I love your huge cock in me!"

I was very excited and released myself inside him. Bradley screamed out, "You're the best when you make love to me, babe!"

I turned over on my back and glanced over towards the door, where I saw the three naked men from the pool staring and grinning at us. I was shocked and confused. What the hell were they doing in our room? I pulled the covers over my head and said, "How did you guys get in here?"

One of the guys said, "We had an invite."

I grabbed the covers from the bed and wrapped them around my body. Then I said, "The show is over, fellas. Please get out of our room, now."

The guys were laughing and said, "Thanks for the show, guys!"

I slammed the door and glared over at Bradley. I asked, "What was *that* all about, Bradley?"

He said, "I just wanted them to know you were taken, hands off."

I said, "So, you invited those men into our room so they could watch us make love?"

He said, "Honey, I love you, and I just don't want a bunch of gay men to think you're available."

I ran into the bathroom and shouted, "You are sick, Bradley!"

I got into the shower and felt sick to my stomach. Bradley came into the bathroom and got into the shower with me. I said, "Bradley, please leave me alone. I don't want to be around you right now."

He pushed me down to the floor of the tub. He said, "What did I do?"

I said, "Bradley, I don't like the way you've been acting and I particularly don't like what just happened."

He got down on the floor of the tub and started to cry. He said, "Honey, I'm sorry for hurting you and for having those guys come into our room. I've never had a boyfriend as hot as you, and I thought you were going to leave me for someone else."

Bradley was sobbing in the shower as he held onto me. I said, "It will be alright. It was just weird. I'm not used to being on display when making love."

He cried more and said, "Please hold me, Patrick. I love you and want you in my life." I held him on the floor of the tub as he was shaking and crying; I felt responsible for making him feel better. This was me – doing it again – living for someone else. I felt obligated to help him. He was a lost soul, and it was *my* duty to help him. Or, so I imagined.

Chapter 13
Coming Out

When I returned home from the trip, I was troubled. First of all, my family thought I was on a business trip the whole time. I had told Tyrone I was going on the trip, but I was afraid to tell him what actually happened. Tyrone is over-protective of me, and I knew if I told him what had occurred, he would level with me. But, how could I explain what had happened to me? It didn't even make sense to *me*.

I wasn't even sure why I continued my relationship with Bradley. He needed me. That was it. He was a 'child' in need of protection, and I was his guardian. No one had reached out to me when I was raped, because I had remained silent. No one knew the horror I had hidden deep down inside. Bradley *was* reaching out to me and telling me he needed me. In my other gay relationships, the guys did not need me to take care of them. They took care of me. Now, I was taking care of someone: Bradley.

I tried to explain this twisted relationship to Tyrone, but he thought I was nuts and couldn't understand why I had pursued a relationship with someone from a distant city. I couldn't understand either.

After the trip to Vegas, Bradley routinely started calling me 'honey' and 'babe.' He became very clingy and needy, and I started to feel like I was in this to help him, only. Bradley didn't seem to have anyone else in his life, and he needed me to make his life feel complete. Or, at least less empty.

Over the next few weeks Bradley called me several times a day. He kept telling me how much he missed me and how he needed to see me more. I occasionally had to travel to Santa Monica for work and told him we could see each other then. Bradley would meet me at my hotel in Santa Monica and stay with me when I was there. It did feel good to be together and the sex was amazing.

One day while we were driving to dinner in downtown Santa Monica, Bradley asked me about my religion. He asked me what I thought about God and what growing up Catholic meant to me. I told him that my religion and faith in God are key focuses in my life. I also explained to him how I felt about my life as a Catholic. I did not tell him about my OCD and its relationship to my acting out various religious rituals.

Bradley told me that he was raised Jewish but never actually practiced his religion. He reminded me that he had attended Catholic masses as a youth and loved the way priests preached the 'good news.' Bradley also told me about his life growing up. He said his father was mean to him and hit him often. He said that his father hit his mother often, as well. After he finally went off to college his mother left his father and sought a divorce. His father then moved to London for his job and married his third wife. She was three years younger than Bradley.

Bradley explained that he had no relationship with his father anymore and that his father never accepted the fact that he was gay. After the divorce, Bradley's mom moved back to Canada. Bradley suffered a lot of pain from his relationship with his father, but he wouldn't talk about it, so I let it go.

When I returned to Chicago, Bradley called me and told me he was falling in love with me. He said he needed to leave California because he no longer liked his life there. Bradley then told me he wanted to move to Chicago. I was stunned and replied, "Bradley, I care a lot about you as well, but you should not move to Chicago just for me."

Bradley said that he had wanted to leave California for a long time and that Chicago would be a good city for him to start the business he'd always dreamt of starting: to shop for all the fashion needs of wealthy women who lacked a refined sense of style.

"Bradley, what about your real estate career?" I asked.

He said, "Patrick, I can do them both. I really want to start a new life, in a new city, with the man I love."

Again I said to Bradley, "If you want to move, do it for yourself. If it doesn't work between us you'll have regrets."

Bradley asked me, "Do you mind if I come out to Chicago in two weeks to explore my moving there?"

I said to him, "You know that you are welcome to come and visit and stay with me ... but think about this first, because it's a big step."

He said, "Honey, you are the greatest. I cannot wait to come see you again in Chicago!"

Bradley flew in on a Friday for one week. I thought it was a crazy idea but it was his life and I couldn't really control him. It's ironic how I allowed so many others to step in and control my life, but I couldn't control someone else's life.

Admittedly, I was very impressed with Bradley that week because he planned everything perfectly. He met with his best friend, Beth, who promised to help him get his business off the ground and introduce him to her rich, socialite friends. Beth told Bradley her friends would love to use his services. At that end of that week, Bradley was determined not only to move to Chicago but also to try to make his dream business come true. I still wasn't convinced this was a good idea. Bradley also spent time that week with a real estate agent looking at condos in the area where I lived.

I went with Bradley and his real estate agent to this new condo only four blocks from my place. The place was lovely, with two bedrooms and two baths. It had a fireplace, hardwood floors, and a nice balcony in back. Bradley said, "Out of all the places I've seen I like this place best. And honey, it's only four blocks from your place. This way you can have your space and we will still be near each other, so we can spend time together."

I said, "Bradley, it is a lovely place, but I think you should move in with me and get your career settled before you buy a new place."

Bradley told his real estate agent that he was very interested and wanted to put a bid on the place. He told the agent he'd call her when he returned to Los Angeles; they could then work out the details. For some reason, I assumed Bradley knew what he was doing and could afford this major undertaking.

Over the next few weeks, as usual, Bradley called me every day. He told me that he was going to put a bid on the condo and move to Chicago the next month. Again I said, "Bradley, are you really serious about this? This is a big move for you. You've lived in Los Angeles for twelve years, now."

Bradley said, "Honey, this is what I want. I want to fulfill my dream by starting my own business and being with the man I love."

It seemed strange to me that I still hadn't told him I loved him. I was uncomfortable with the situation. It all was happening too fast and I couldn't control any of it.

Bradley put an offer on the condo at and his offer was accepted. What I didn't know was how Bradley was going to pay for the place. Again, I just assumed he had the money. One Saturday night I was on the Foster bus heading towards Andersonville to meet Tyrone and Rico for dinner and drinks when my phone rang; it was Bradley. He was crying and upset. I said, "What's wrong? Did something happen?"

Bradley said, "My father is an ass and again he is making my life a living hell."

I said to Bradley, "I thought you didn't talk to your father."

He said, "I normally don't but I called him a few weeks ago and asked him if he could lend me $80,000 dollars to put a deposit on the condo." Bradley told me his father gave him the money out of guilt. He got the check and immediately deposited into his bank account.

Actually, Bradley had lied to his father and told him he was buying a place in California. This is why his father agreed to the loan. But what actually happened is that Bradley's father called his brother Ivan, who lives in Canada. Ivan told his father that Bradley was using the money to buy a place in Chicago. Ivan also told him about us. Apparently, Bradley's father got upset and demanded the money back. Then Bradley called me crying, not knowing what to do.

I said, "Listen, just give the money back to your dad and do things on your own."

Bradley said, "I need his money or I can't buy the place in Chicago."

I said, "Bradley, why did you rely on your father for the down payment? You have no relationship with him."

He said, "My father is a bastard. He owes me for everything he did to me while I was growing up. Ivan told him about you and me and that's why he won't let me keep the money. I am not going to give him the money back. I already deposited it in my bank account."

I said, "Bradley, I am here for you but I am getting off the bus right now to meet Tyrone and Rico for dinner."

Bradley said, "So, Tyrone and Rico are more important than your boyfriend?"

I said, "Bradley, I want to help you and we can talk later, but now my friends are waiting for me."

He said, "Go ahead, have fun with your friends, I'll call you later."

When I got into the restaurant, Tyrone and Rico were seated at the table. Tyrone could tell something was wrong. He said, "What's going on, bud? You look upset."

I said, "I just got off the phone with Bradley and he's a mess." Then, I told them the whole story.

Tyrone looked at me and said, "Bud, this guy has not even moved here yet and he's bringing drama into your life. You don't need this bullshit. You have a good life, and I am just saying I would dump his ass."

I said, "Tyrone, Bradley and I have been dating long distance for a year. Why would I just dump him now?"

Tyrone said, "There is just something about this guy I do not like, Patrick."

I said, "Tyrone, you do not even know him and you are already judging him."

Tyrone said, "He is too much in your face and you deserve better, Patrick. Dump him before you get hurt."

I said, "I'm a big boy and can take care of myself, thank you."

Tyrone said, "You put yourself out there for everyone and at the end of the day, you pay for other people's problems. Honestly Patrick, I do not even know why you are getting yourself involved with this guy. I say you toss him to the curb."

I said, "Come on Tyrone, can't you give the guy a chance?"

Tyrone peered into my eyes and said, "Patrick, mark my words: this guy is trouble."

The following week Bradley called and told me his father had hired an attorney to take him to court to get his $80,000 back. I said, "Bradley, just give your dad the money back and move to Chicago and live with me until you get situated."

Bradley said, "I have a plan and it will be okay." Then he asked, "Can you promise to help me and be at my side."

I said, "Bradley, I will do what I can, but you really have to think about what you're doing here."

A few days later Bradley actually gave the money back to his father. He said he talked to his mother and she offered to give him

$6,000 dollars to help him with his down payment. It was a long way from $80,000, but if he could get another $6,000 he could afford to make his monthly mortgage payments.

Bradley asked me, "Patrick, how much money do you have saved in the bank?"

I said, "I have $8,000 dollars."

He said, "Could you loan me $6,000 and I'll promise to pay you back within six months?"

I said, "Bradley, do you know how long it took me to save that money?"

I told him the money is not just mine; it is also for Cynthia's future. "Listen," I said. "I do not think it's a good idea for you to buy this place. I have told you that you can come live with me rent-free until you get your business started."

Bradley responded, "I want this place and my mother is going to help me. I just need your help, too. Patrick, I promise I will pay you back every cent."

I said, "Bradley, this is my life savings and money doesn't grow on trees for me."

He pleaded with me, "I will pay you back the $6,000 plus interest within six months."

I said, "I am not feeling comfortable with this, Bradley."

"Patrick, I love you and I need your help. Please lend me the money and I will pay you back."

I gave in. "Fine, I'll lend you the money, but I must have it back in six months, no longer," I said. I'm not sure *what* I was thinking. I had been dating this guy long-distance for a year, but there was still so much I didn't know about him. What was I doing loaning all this money to him?

Bradley was going to be leaving Los Angeles for good the first week of September. In his last month in LA, he sold all of his belongings but his clothes. He packed up his car, including his dogs, and started his long journey to Chicago. He made it to Las Vegas when his car overheated and broke down. Bradley called me at that point and he was very upset. He said, "It's 115 degrees in Las Vegas and I don't know what to do with the dogs. I need to get to a hotel where I can get the dogs into air conditioning and get my car fixed."

Bradley needed to be in Chicago in three days in order to close on his condo. He told me, "I'm going to leave the car in Las Vegas to be fixed and then have it shipped to Chicago."

He decided to rent a car and drive the rest of the way to

Chicago. He said the rental car service would not accept his credit card and so he needed to use mine. I said, "Bradley, what is it going to cost me to have you rent a car from Las Vegas?"

He replied, "Patrick, it will only be a few hundred dollars, and I promise to pay you back when I give you back the $6,000. Patrick, please do this for me. I need to be in Chicago for my condo signing in three days."

I said, "Fine Bradley, here's my credit card information. This move has been way too much for me to handle, though."

Bradley replied, "Honey, it will all be okay when I get there and we're together."

Suddenly, I wondered what in the world I was doing. My life was fine a year ago, and now I'm taking care of a grown man who I'm not sure I even love.

Bradley arrived in Chicago a mere twelve hours before the signing of his condo. I had been with this man for less than a year and he'd already cost me nearly $7,000. I was nervous about where this relationship was taking me. Bradley and the dogs stayed with me until his move-in date. During that time all the craziness of Bradley's move settled and we started to enjoy one another's company again. Somehow, it was all becoming very real.

We spent every day together. The life that I once had alone was now filled with a partner and someone who needed me to take care of him. It was much different when Alberto moved in because he was taking care of *me*. There were so many times that I wanted to end things, though, because the relationship was really not working for me. The key problem here was that Bradley owed me about $7,000, and I just couldn't walk away from that. That money was my and Cynthia's future. Bradley used his large debt to me to his advantage.

Now that we were living in the same city, Bradley became an intimate part of my life. Though, at times, I felt like I was suffocating. Bradley demanded to become involved in every facet of my life. This created problems because I had still not come out of the closet to my family or the people at work. I had obligations to my family. My father was ill. My mother needed me around and I wanted to be there to help her. I could not even do that alone because Bradley needed to be involved, as well.

My mother started a family tradition a few years back that every Thursday evening my sister Gabriella, my brother Marco, and I would get together at her house for dinner. Bradley demanded that I bring him the next time around because he wanted so badly to be a part of my family life. I brought him with me the next Thursday and introduced him as my friend who had just moved here from LA. My family knew something was up because Bradley was very self-absorbed and it was obvious that he was openly gay. Still, I begged him not to tell my family. I told him I would do that when the time was right.

One night when we came home from dinner at my mother's Bradley said, "I love your family as much as I love you. I want them to know about us and accept the fact that we're lovers."

I said, "Bradley, it's very hard for me to discuss my sexuality with my family, and I'm not sure I'm ready to do that."

Bradley said, "You told me all about your pathetic episodes with Marty and Alberto, and I am not going to be any part of that. Either you tell your family or I'll do it for us."

I'm not sure why, but I decided that the first person in my family I would come out to as a gay man would be my sister, Maria. Maria and I had grown apart over the years because she decided to distance herself from the family when Dad became ill. She did not want to help in assisting with my father's illness. Maria had become consumed with her own life and wanted no part in our family, anymore. We had not actually talked in about a year but because her husband's brother was gay, I figured they would accept me and understand my decision to come out to them. I called Maria and asked if she and Steve could meet me for dinner. Maria accepted my invite having no idea of the bomb I was about to drop on her.

We met at a restaurant, and when Bradley and I walked in together they seemed somewhat confused. I introduced Bradley to them and we sat down. I told them the two of us had met when I was on a business trip in California. I explained that Bradley had just moved to Chicago and that I was introducing him to new people so he could become comfortable with the city.

After a few glasses of wine, I started to feel more comfortable with Bradley being with me. During the course of the dinner, Bradley excused himself and said he needed to use the restroom. While he was gone from the table, I looked at Maria and Steve and said, "I have something important to tell you."

They both looked at me intensely. Maria said, "What's wrong?" I said, "I am telling the both of you this because I feel you can understand and respect my decision."

Maria said, "We're family, tell us what you need to tell us,

Patrick."

I said, "I haven't told anyone in our family this and I need to ask you both to not say a word until I have told the rest of the family."

I could tell by the look on their faces that they knew what I was going to say. Bradley returned to the table and I took his hand and looked at Maria and Steve and said, "This is my boyfriend." Bradley looked at me and smiled. Maria and Steve had huge smiles on their faces and both got up and hugged me.

Maria said, "I knew for years, but was waiting for you to tell us, Patrick. It was obvious, but you just held it inside."

Steve, who is a wonderful human being said, "Patrick, I am so proud of you and just want you to be happy."

I looked at Maria and said, "Please do not say a word. I want Mom and Dad to find out from me."

Bradley was beaming with excitement and said, "I'm so excited to be a part of your family."

My sister Maria said, "Bradley, be careful what you ask for with our family, because you know they're all crazy."

I said, "Maria, listen I know we have had our differences over the years, but I love our family and do not want you to fill Bradley's head with things you are bitter over."

Maria hugged Bradley and said, "I am happy for you and happy for Patrick, and you are always welcome into our home." Then Maria said, "Don't expect that to be the case with the *rest* of our family, though."

I said, "Maria, it will be alright. I'm going to tell everyone when I'm ready." We ended the night on a good note and promised we would get together soon.

I had finally done it. I had come out of the closet to a family member. This was a huge step for me, and I was nervous. How would I approach the rest of my family about this, though? Would they be as accepting as Maria and Steve? Would I become the scandal of our family? The last thing in the world I wanted to do was hurt or disappoint my family. I love them, and they are my life. Why did I decide *now* to come out to them? I had so many questions running through my head I couldn't think straight.

A few days later I got a phone call from my mother and she said, "I need to speak with you. Can you come over tonight?"

I said, "Is something wrong, Mom?"

She said, "No, I just need to talk with you."

This was not like my mother, because when she has something

on her mind she just lets it out. She knew something. Maria must have told her. What was I going to do?

I went over to Mom's house and she was sitting alone in the kitchen. I said, "What's up? Where's Dad?"

Mom said, "Your brother took Dad with him so he could get out of the house."

I said, "What did you want to talk to me about, Mom?"

She said, "I was talking to your Aunt Jessica and she told me something."

I said, "Okay. What did Aunt Jessica tell you?"

Mom said, "My sister told me she found out that you are gay."

My heart dropped to the floor. I could see the disappointment in Mom's eyes. I said, "What are you talking about, Mom?" I was frozen. I didn't know what else to say.

Mom said, "Patrick, is it true?"

I said, "Mom, I've wanted to tell you for a long time."

Mom said, "Patrick, *is it true*? Are you really gay?"

With tears running down my face, I said, "Mom, yes, I am gay."

Mom walked over to the sink and began to wash dishes. I said, "Mom, stop washing dishes and look at me."

Mom said, "I do not believe you're gay. You were married to two women and have children."

I said, "Mom, I have been carrying this with me for a long time."

Mom said, "How is it that my *sister* tells me my son is gay? Who else have you told this to, Patrick?"

I said, "Mom, the only person I have told is Maria."

"You tell your sister who has distanced herself from this family? You go tell her that you think you're gay before telling anyone else. *Why?*" she pleaded.

"First of all, Mom, I *am* gay and I told Maria because I thought she and Steve

would understand because Steve's brother Arthur is gay," I replied.

Mom had her hands in a sink full of suds washing the dishes. She looked at me and declared, "My baby boy is not gay. This is a phase in your life, Patrick. You were married to bad women who did not treat you right. You will find a nice girl and get married again and live a happy life." Mom said all of this as if reading from a how-to manual.

I said, "Mom, I have tried that and it didn't work. I want to be with a man, now. I have always kept these feelings deep inside so that no one in the family would be hurt. I'm done hiding now. I'm with Bradley."

Mom said, "I love you more than anything in the world, Patrick, and you are always welcome in my home, but I will not believe that you are gay."

I said, "Mom, I can only tell you the way I feel and that I want you to be a part of my life."

Suddenly, I heard my brother Marco coming in the back door and helping my dad up the stairs. When Dad got to the top of the stairs, I pulled him into the kitchen and Marco handed me Dad's walker. I sat Dad down in a chair in the kitchen. I was about to tell him my secret, but before I could speak a word Mom said, "Patrick, you need to be on your way. I have to feed your father lunch."

Dad said, "Patrick, why are you here today?"

Mom interrupted and said, "He was checking up on you, Butch. Now, Patrick, you need to be on your way."

She had tears in her eyes. I felt like I had just shattered her world. I said, "Mom, are you going to be okay?"

Mom kissed me on the cheek and said, "Honey, I love you and I am fine. Now go, be on your way." I left the house. I had just come out to my mom. I felt lost.

I came home to Bradley's and he said, "How did it go with your mother?"

I said, "She doesn't believe it."

Bradley said, "Give her time. It will be fine."

Then Bradley said, "By the way, *my* mom is coming and I invited her to your mother's for Thanksgiving."

I said, "Bradley, we should have talked about this *before* you invited your mother to my parents."

Bradley snapped, "Patrick, get over it and be a man. I am tired of pretending to please your family. They need to deal with the situation and accept me as your lover once and for all."

Why did I continue to allow this man so much influence over my life? I became so overwhelmed by my feelings of entrapment that I walked into the bedroom and cried from sheer frustration. I know that Bradley could hear me crying, but he just went about his business. Maybe he found satisfaction in my suffering. Whatever the case, I felt horribly alone and ashamed, the same frozen emotions I'd experienced so long ago on the cold floor of a Goldblatt's men's room.

That night I also became very upset with my sister, Maria. I needed to confront her and let her know how much she'd hurt me by spilling my secret to our mother. I called her, and I could tell she was uneasy talking to me. I said, "Maria, I was at Mom and Dad's today. Mom told me she found out I was gay from Aunt Jessica."

Maria said, "Patrick, I'm so sorry. I was so happy when you told me, and I was a little drunk when Steve and I got home. I am very close to Aunt Jessica and it just came out in our conversation."

I said, "Maria, I confided in you. I told you something I'd never told anyone else."

Maria started crying and said, "Patrick, please don't be upset with me. I didn't mean to tell Aunt Jessica, and I never thought she would tell Mom. Please Patrick, don't hate me. I'm the only one in the family that will truly accept you for being gay."

I said, "Maria, I love you, but you disappointed me once again. First, you reject your family because you do not want to deal with your father's illness. Then you exploit my being gay to our Aunt. You must have known it would get back to Mom. What is it that makes you want to hurt Mom and Dad and me?"

"Patrick, I will stand by you, I promise," she pleaded.

I said, "Maria, I am really disappointed in you. Right now, I really need to think about what you did to me."

For the most part, that ended the relationship between my sister and me. It's not that I don't forgive her for betraying me. It's because she's shown so little respect for either me or our parents over the years.

*****

By now, Bradley and I were living in our own homes but spending every day together. I went to work every day and, upon returning home, I'd change into my gym clothes and go over to Bradley's place to be with him. Bradley started to plead with me to put my place up for sale or rent it in order to move in with him. But I told him that I still needed my own space. To this, Bradley said, "If you really love me, Patrick, you'll move in with me."

It had already been two months since Bradley moved to Chicago, and I was spending all my free time with him. I cooked our meals, did the laundry, took the dogs out, and did all I could to please Bradley. He seemed happy as he could be, but I found myself living a lie once again. I enjoyed being gay and having a relationship with a man, but there were still so many things that I could not understand about Bradley. There was a big part of him that, in my gut, I just didn't trust.

*****

One night we invited Tyrone over for dinner. We were sitting in the dining room eating a pot roast I had made and drinking wine. At one point, Bradley started to insult me and then told Tyrone that I was coward because I wouldn't stand up to my family and tell them all I was gay. Bradley told Tyrone he was going to 'change me' and make me the gay man I needed to be. I became so uncomfortable that I got up quietly and carried some dishes into the kitchen.

As I stood at the dishwasher loading dishes into it, Tyrone shouted over to me saying, "Are you going to let this guy say these things about you, Patrick?"

I replied, "Tyrone, have a drink, it's fine."

Tyrone stood up, glared at Bradley and said, "Patrick and I have been through a lot. He's my best friend. You will *not* talk to him that way. You're an *asshole*, Bradley. Apologize to my friend right now!"

I turned to Tyrone and said, "It's fine. Sit down, please."

Tyrone said, "No, Patrick, I will not sit down. You have dated two amazing guys that you let go, and this asshole comes into your life and you allow him to treat you this way?"

Bradley got up and said, "Who are you calling an asshole?"

Tyrone said, "*You* are an asshole. You will not treat my best friend this way."

Bradley was drunk. He looked over at me and said, "Honey, come over and give me a kiss."

Tyrone said, "Patrick, if you kiss this asshole, I'm out of here."

Bradley looked at Tyrone and said, "Don't let the door hit you on the way out."

Tyrone grabbed his jacket, scowled at Bradley, and said, "Bitch, you do *not* know who you are dealing with."

Then, Tyrone took off down the stairs. I chased after him and stopped him in the hallway at the bottom of the stairs. Tyrone said, "What the hell are you doing with this loser, Patrick? Go upstairs, get your jacket, and let's go to Boystown for drinks."

I said, "I can't just leave him Tyrone, we're in a relationship."

Tyrone said, "What's with you? I've seen you with a lot of good guys. Why are you with *him*?"

I said, "I have more invested than you understand, Tyrone."

He asked, "Patrick, what did you do for this guy? What is holding you back from leaving?"

I said, "Tyrone, I cannot get into this right now."

Tyrone said, "I love you, Patrick, and you are like my brother, but I cannot deal with that asshole. I will not listen to him talk to you the way he does." He then stormed out the door.

I walked back up the stairs. Bradley was standing in the doorway. When I reached the top, he grabbed me by my hair and threw me to the floor.

He said, "I heard everything that motherfucker said about me. Do you want to go out with that fucker and find some guy to screw?"

I said, "Bradley, I'm back here with you. Why are you doing this?"

Bradley leaned down and slapped my face, and I started bleeding from my mouth. I wanted to get up and defend myself but what would that solve? Bradley yelled, "Get your pathetic ass up and clean the kitchen!"

At that moment, I was once again reliving the rape. I had let this man verbally and physically abuse me. I couldn't understand what I was doing anymore. I realized that Bradley had $7,000 hanging over my head. If I left him, I would never see a penny of the money I'd saved so long for Cynthia and me. I felt cornered, isolated. I cried myself to sleep that night and kept praying to God to free me from this terrible affliction.

*****

The weekends I had Cynthia became difficult for me. Bradley wanted us to appear as this loving, gay couple for Cynthia. I had never told Cynthia I was gay, but I figured she probably knew by now. I'd always wanted to protect her from hearing me say, *"I'm gay,"* as if saying this was something to be ashamed of. But, I was still not ready to have Cynthia accept my being gay. This was my little girl and I wanted her to first accept Bradley as my friend. In time, I would explain to her that Bradley and I were a couple and go from there.

But things between Bradley and Cynthia were not harmonious. Cynthia couldn't understand Bradley's inflated personality or his odd behaviors. I tried to keep the two of them apart, but Bradley wanted us to be a family. Cynthia really did not want to be friends with Bradley, let alone be a pretend family.

Bradley made things seem so forced and artificial.

One Thursday after work, I went home to pick up Bradley to go to my parent's house for dinner. When I came into the house, for no particular reason, Bradley started accusing me of cheating on him. He said he saw an email of mine from my friend, Stanley. Bradley demanded to know who Stanley was and I told him that he was just a friend that used to hang out with Tyrone and me. Bradley again accused me of cheating and hit me and told me to stop lying to him. When he struck me, I fell onto the table and cut my face. I got up, grabbed my jacket, and ran out the door. Bradley ran after me and started pleading with me to forgive him. He screamed that he was sorry he'd hit me. I decided to let it go and told him to get in the car. Then, we drove over to my parent's house for dinner.

When we walked in, Mom said, "Patrick, I made your favorite dinner. Sit down before it gets cold." Bradley and I grabbed a seat and we all began to eat.

Then Mom looked at me and said, "What happened to your face, Patrick?"

My sister Gabriella looked at me and said, "You have a black eye, Patrick. What happened?"

But before I could speak, Bradley interrupted and said, "Your brother was sleepwalking the other night and walked into the bedroom door."

I didn't say a word but I could feel the tension growing at the table. My family obviously wasn't buying Bradley's version of the story. Bradley continued saying, "Your brother is a big, clumsy fool."

My mother looked up and said, "Don't you ever call my son a clumsy fool." Mom looked into my eyes, and then grabbed her plate and put it into the sink.

When I got home that night Bradley said, "You are such a momma's boy."

I said, "Bradley, please do not start with my family, because they will always defend me."

I was starting to feel like a cornered animal and just wanted to escape. All I could think of was that I would never get back the money I had given to this guy. I also thought that I had come out to my family for this guy, and it was a very bad relationship. Would they judge me because I had made yet another huge mistake?

A few weeks later, I found a couple to rent my condo, and I

moved in with Bradley. Now I was living a life I simply could not understand. I had always had the courage to pick up and move on when life became too much for me to handle. I stayed with Bradley, in part, because he owed me so much money and I thought by staying with him, he would eventually pay me back. Unfortunately, Bradley wasn't even making enough money to pay his own bills, let alone making enough to pay off a sizeable loan. So, I started paying his mortgage and buying all of our food. Now Bradley was completely dependent on me to get by.

One day, Bradley asked me to lend him my credit card so he could pick up things we needed for the house. Without thinking, I handed him my card. When I got my next credit card statement in the mail, I noticed some unusual charges and asked Bradley about it. He said, "I picked up a couple of cute outfits that will fit both of us."

"Bradley, I don't use my credit cards unless I have no money left," I told him.

He said, "Are you saying you don't trust your boyfriend?"

"It's not that I don't trust you, Bradley, but I have to watch what we spend," I replied.

Bradley said, "I will take care of things. You have nothing to worry about."

I became more and more depressed in the coming days. Everyone that loved me could tell that I was no longer myself. One day I was on a Blue Line train heading in to work. Usually I took the Brown Line, but for some reason this day I went to the Irving Park stop and boarded the train. As I sat on the train, I leaned my head back and closed my eyes for a few minutes.

When we got to the next stop, I lifted my head up and opened my eyes. I looked around the train and across the aisle from me was this older gentleman wearing a baseball cap. I kept looking at him because I recognized his face from somewhere; I just couldn't place him. I continued staring at this man, trying to figure out how I knew him. Then, he started looking over at me, and suddenly it dawned on me how I knew him. We made eye contact and both of us smiled. I said, "Bob Redman." He replied, "Pat Dati." We laughed and I moved over to sit next to him.

Bob and I had worked together about ten years ago at Chicago Financial Publishing. Bob was an editor in our publishing department and I worked in marketing. Bob is a fabulous guy who is well-liked by everyone in the company. He possesses the classic 'heart of gold' and is gentle and kind in manner. We talked all the way downtown and both of us almost missed our stops. When we parted, Bob offered me his business card and urged me to call him in order to get caught up with one another. I assured Bob that I would follow up and told him how great it was to have run into him that day.

I thought about Bob for the rest of the day. He really made an impact on me. I remembered that Bob was gay and had lived with his partner for nearly forty years. The two of them had actually lived not far from my condo and had a beautiful home. I knew this about Bob, because my friend Jack still worked with Bob and they had become good friends. It was fate that connected Bob Redman and me that day.

The following week Bradley's mother, Helen, came in for Thanksgiving and stayed with us. We brought Helen to my parents' house on Thanksgiving Day and she had a wonderful time. Everyone accepted Helen and made her feel comfortable. She is a lovely woman with a warm smile and a sort of peace to her.

The next day we were going to take Helen shopping in the city but decided to take her for breakfast first. While Helen was getting ready, I decided to take the dogs out as we were going to be gone for several hours. I threw on Bradley's winter jacket as I normally would for a cold, wintry morning. When I returned, Helen was ready to go. We were just waiting for Bradley to come out of the bedroom.

When Bradley emerged from the bedroom, he sneered at me and said, "What the fuck do you think you're doing with my jacket on?"

Helen looked at Bradley and said, "Don't talk to Patrick that way."

I said, "Bradley, I just put your jacket on to take the dogs out. I'll take it off if it's going to make you mad."

Helen looked at me and said, "Patrick, do *not* take that jacket off, let's leave."

Bradley looked at both of us and said, "If he doesn't take my jacket off, then I am not going."

I looked at Bradley and finally felt safe to say what I felt. I knew he would not hit me in front of his mother. I said, "Bradley, fuck you. I'm wearing the jacket."

Helen smiled at me and said, "Patrick, you are a saint. I do not know why you put up with my son's bullshit."

Helen and I walked down to the car and got in. Bradley then

came running down and stood in front of the car with his arms crossed in front of his chest. Helen was sitting in the passenger seat and looked over at me and said, "Why are you with my son if he treats you this way, Patrick?" Then she rolled down her window and shouted, "Bradley, get out of the way or I will go back upstairs and leave right now." Bradley walked around the car and got into the back seat. We never talked about that episode again.

*****

Bradley's 40th birthday was coming up and he planned a huge celebration. He told me since it was his 40th birthday he wanted to go to Texas and celebrate with his friends from high school. Then he wanted to go to Las Vegas with Beth and Walter. Finally, he wanted us to go to Canada to celebrate with his family.

I said, "Bradley, I cannot afford all these trips. You still owe me $7,000, remember?"

Bradley said, "Patrick, you are the love of my life. I am not doing this for me; I want you to meet all the important people in my life. I want them to see the man I love. I am such a part of your life, why do you not want to be a part of mine?"

I said, "Bradley, how can we afford these trips? I am the only one working and I'm paying both mortgages."

Bradley said, "Honey, my business is starting to pick up. I am doing work for Beth and some of her friends, and they are paying me cash." Then he said, "We can charge the trips on your credit card and I will make the payment."

I said, "Bradley, I am not comfortable with that."

He said, "Do you not love me, Patrick? Please, I promise I'll pay you back."

Of course, he never did.

*****

What I thought would be the final straw happened one Sunday when Bradley and I were getting my condo ready to show to a potential renter. Along the way, we got into a fight on my back porch. After Bradley shouted something and I yelled back, he pushed me down the porch stairs. I lay at the bottom of the stairs and knew something was very wrong. I couldn't get up. I yelled for Bradley but he didn't come. Then someone from the building next door heard me screaming and came to help. The guy asked if I was okay. I told him, "I can't move, I can't get up."

The neighbor called 911 and an ambulance sped me to the emergency room. Bradley followed in his car. I learned I had fractured my arm and would need surgery to place a pin in it. I wouldn't tell anyone how it happened, though. Bradley felt so bad, he took care of me and did everything I asked of him. I couldn't tell my family about the incident because I was afraid what they would do to him. When people at work asked what happened, I just told them I'd fallen down my back stairs.

After this incident, things got so bad that I became suicidal. One day, I took a handful of my antidepressants and drove down a side street while calling friends I hadn't spoken to in months. Everyone was worried about me and begged me to get help. I called Bradley and told him I wanted to die. Bradley said, "I am so over your drama, Patrick. I'm shopping for a client right now and don't have time for your crazy bullshit." He hung up on me.

Next, I called my sister Gabriella and told her I was going to end my life. I'd had enough and could no longer deal with my life. Gabriella gave the phone to my goddaughter Joann to talk with me. Gabriella then grabbed her house phone and called Bradley. Bradley answered the phone and Gabriella shouted, "Where are you? My brother is trying to take his life!"

Bradley said, "I am over your brother's drama and he's just crying wolf."

My sister said, "You son of a bitch! That's my brother and he is your partner. If anything happens to my brother, let me tell you, I will kill you with my own hands. You'd better find Patrick and get him home or I will hunt you down, Bradley!"

Bradley called my phone as I was sitting a few blocks from the house and out of my mind on medication. I said, "Bradley, leave me alone to die, just leave me alone."

Bradley said, "Tell me where you are, Patrick. Everyone is looking for you."

I said, "I will come home."

I am not sure how I drove those few blocks because I was crying so hard. When I got home, Bradley beat me until my entire body hurt. I pulled myself off the ground and waited for Bradley to leave.

Once he was gone, I called my psychiatrist and told him what was happening. He said, "Patrick, call someone in your family to pick you up or I will call the police."

I called my mother and asked her to pick me up. I walked out of Bradley's place in a daze and found my mother waiting for me.

Mom looked at me and jumped out of the car. She yelled, "Patrick, what happened to you!"

I said, "Mom, please just take me home."

I was bleeding and bruised all over my body. My psychiatrist called and asked to speak with my mother. He told my mom to take me to the hospital. My mom said, "No, I am taking my son home to my house."

The doctor said, "Your son has tried to commit suicide."

My mom said, "He's okay. I have him now and he'll be okay."

The next day my doctor admitted me to an outpatient mental health program. I spent the entire next month in a psychiatric ward discussing my state of mind and attempts to commit suicide. I told the doctors that my life meant nothing to me anymore, and I no longer wanted to live. I could barely function anymore. Even Wendy was concerned about me because she knew Cynthia was aware of my state of mind.

I knew it was time to leave Bradley, once and for all. I came to realize that my relationship with him was not unlike the attack I had experienced as a child. Bradley was 'raping' me over and over, and I stayed because I was a victim; a role I knew all too well at this point in my life. I wrote Bradley the following letter to end our relationship:

Dear Bradley,

I am writing this letter to tell you my true feelings and to release the anxiety I have been holding within for way too long. I am exhausted and need to rest. I am not angry, mad, jealous, or confused. I want to live again. I cannot live with abuse and pain any more.

You have been a very important person in my life. Meeting you has been something God meant to happen. I was living my life for many years lost, confused, and afraid to be myself. Then you came into my life and opened me up, so I could find myself.

But I have come to realize that we are two very different people. They say opposites attract and, while that may be so, we are truly moving in different directions at this time. The comment my sister Gabriella made to me about us not being right for each other shocked me at first, but I came to realize it was true. Gabriella loves me as does the rest of my family, but she is particularly concerned for me. She has seen me through so many troubled times and just wants me to be happy. I have been fighting depression for so long. My depression comes from the abuse I have experienced as a child and as an adult, including the abuse in our relationship.

The happiest time over the last 8 years was back in 2004. Although I was still hiding my real self, I was living my life for once on my own. I bought my first home, to live in alone. It was fun decorating my home my way. I was able to bring Cynthia to a place that was our home together. I developed new friends who were different from the friends I had in the past. These new friends were people that took me under their wings and made me laugh, something that I hadn't done in years. I deserved this time to myself, because for so long I lived my life for other people, rarely thinking about myself. I lived my life to be who they wanted me to be; I hid the me I truly am. I AM ME!

I admit I have problems. I am dependent on anti-depression drugs. I have low self-esteem. I allow people to take advantage of me. I tried attempting suicide twice. I give too much, and I don't let people give back. All of these problems I'll try to deal with, in time. Maybe I can become a happy person again.

I need time to get myself together, because right now I am like a scattered puzzle - messed up and incomplete. I have all the pieces to the puzzle, and for a time they were almost together, but then they fell apart. This past year was one of the worst years of my life. I was struggling with my career. I was allowing Wendy to use Cynthia to drive me crazy and to dictate when and how I should live my life. Coming out to my family was the most difficult experience of my life and the pressures from it are still making me feel uneasy, even lost. Then, leaving my home and moving in with you made me feel like I'd lost this happy person I became in 2004. I have allowed us to accumulate serious credit card debt – that fact has disturbed and angered me. Finally, I spent last summer in an outpatient mental center due to a nervous breakdown. I even tried to commit suicide.

It amazes me that I made it through this nightmare alive. I have turned some of the negative issues from last year around. I found a new job that I love and find fulfilling. I set Wendy straight and told her I will not allow her to control my life, and I made sure she will not sabotage my relationship with Cynthia. I'm now out and honest with my family and feel more comfortable. I also realize that taking my life would be deeply selfish and leave Cynthia without the father that she loves.

Now, I have to work on the other issues. I need to gain control over my low self-esteem issues. My plan is to spend weeknights roller blading or doing any activity not related to partying. I will party only on weekends that I don't have Cynthia. As for the depression, I soon start my sessions with Dr. Phillip again. With regards to our living arrangements, I need to make some serious decisions. My plan is to rent my place and move back with my parents and pay down my credit card debts. This will not be easy, but I don't have any other option. I realize it's going back a few steps, but it will allow me to get my life back on track.

Leaving this relationship is difficult for me. You have become my best friend, lover, caretaker, and partner. During our 2 ½ years together, we have been through a lot, some good and too much not so good. I think one of the key problems with our relationship is our very different personalities. I'm serious and rarely allow myself to be at ease. You, on the other hand, are very laid back and casual. You appear as if you don't have a care in the world, and if you do, you hide it well. Also, I have shared a lot about myself, and you have kept much of yourself hidden away from me. I worry about what others think and put them before myself. You always put yourself first; everyone else comes at a distant second. We're opposites, Bradley. We hold very different values and beliefs. We grew up in very different worlds.

What does all this mean? It means I need to take care of me for a change. If I am not healthy and happy, I will continue to make the people around me miserable. I want to laugh again. I want to stop crying in bed at night. I want to stop drinking my problems away. I want to take control of my being. The reason I have survived this long is due to God and His plan for me. I am on this earth to do His work and fulfill my mission. I need to get back on track. If I don't get back on track, I'll lose my mind. This depression and anxiety will cause me to have a heart attack or stroke. I watched my father go through this. It runs in my family. I want to live a long and good life. I want to be the best father, son, friend, brother and person I can be. I'm not any of these people today. I feel like a robot with no controls. This is no one's fault but mine, and I'm the only one who can fix it.

I realize that our different personalities and histories often left you frustrated and upset, but I can't live my life anymore letting someone hurt me physically, mentally, and verbally. I need to be in control of my life. I deserve to be with someone who makes me laugh, not cry.

When I read the letter my friend Bob wrote his lover the other night, I cried. His words were so sweet and honest. The words he used to describe his love for his lover amazed me and really made me think: Could I say these words about Bradley? I want the type of love that Bob and his partner have, but apparently it's not the right time for me. I am broken and need to be fixed. I cannot love someone else until I learn to love myself. That is the key problem I face: I do not love myself. I might have at one time, but I allowed the abuse I experienced in life to destroy my ability to love myself.

So ends my story – for now. Right now I am not fit to be in a relationship. I have to take responsibility for fixing my problems and becoming well again. Until I do these things, I can't move on. I wish things were different, but they're not. I wish you well.

Patrick

When I dropped that letter in the mail to Bradley, I knew it was over. I realized that living with more abuse would eventually kill me. This sounds crazy, but leaving Bradley made me feel guilty, somehow. I felt like I deserted a person who needed my help. Now, however, I realize that's the way abused people really think. We try to protect the people who hurt us. We make excuses for why these people have harmed us. We hide and refuse to acknowledge what is happening in our lives. It makes little sense, but we believe that if we just pretend the abuse didn't happen, we are pleasing the people who care about us.

Bradley showed up at my parent's house about a week later and tried to speak with my mother. She told him that if he didn't get off her front stairs, she would 'kick his ass' and call the police. Bradley said, "Mrs. Dati, what did your son tell you? It must have been all lies."

My mother said, "I saw the scars on my son's face, and I'm aware of the financial trouble you have put him in. Bradley, I'm telling you right now, if you so much as call my son again, I will hunt you down and take care of you myself. You do not know who you are messing with, because I will *not* take any of your shit. Go on your way now, before I call the police."

Mom always had a way with words.

Bradley tried calling me at work. I told him that if he kept calling, I was going to have him arrested for harassment. It was hard for me to be so honest, but I could no longer remain dependent upon an abusive person any more. I never recovered any of the money Bradley owed me. He had run up outrageous charges on my credit card, but I had to admit I allowed that to happen.

One day much later, while at a gay bar with friends, Bradley came up to me drunk and put his arms around me, saying, "I love you baby, and cannot live without you."

I said, "Bradley, get away from me right now or I will have you arrested."

It has not been easy putting this complicated puzzle back together. My good friend Bob Redman has taught me many good lessons in life. Perhaps one of his better ones is, *"Pat Dati, just let it go and love will find you."*

It hasn't been easy, of course, but I have escaped another abusive person, and I'm living my life again. I still have my family and good friends who have given me the courage to begin my life again and maybe, just maybe, finally find happiness.

Epilogue
Wake up you sleepy head.
Get Up! Get outta bed.
Live, love, laugh and be happy.

A few years after I left Bradley, I met a man in a gay bar and went home with him. His name is Greg. He's a good man, a kind and gentle man, and a smart man. I know he's smart because my friend Bob knows Greg studied to be a Jesuit, and he told me all Jesuits are smart, not just smart but really smart. Bob was a Franciscan monk. They are not known for being smart. They just love. Bob and Greg have this thing – whether it's better to be smart or loving – going on between them. It makes them laugh a lot together.

Now, Greg and I have been together over a year and I have moved in with him. One night, after someone in my family deliberately hurt me, Greg took me in his arms and said, "You are my love and life now, so listen to what I'm going to say." As I looked into his eyes, he said, "As long as you are with me, no one will ever hurt you again." We're obviously lovers now, and for the first time, I'm ready. I believe for the first time in my life, I'm lovable. I can hardly believe I believe it. I feel like a little boy waking up on a beautiful summer morning.

One night a few months after I had met Greg, I was home

alone and frightened, so I held my prayer book and said the rosary over and over. Then, suddenly I let go. I think I must have thought for a moment about Greg's love for me. This letting go was like being bathed in light. I saw that the OCD was really my inability to let go and be myself, to open up to my true spirit and pray. I prayed as the person I truly am. As I prayed, I realized life is all about forgiving people, including myself, for everything that has happened. I needed to forgive and let people go to be themselves. And I needed, quite simply, to just let me be me.

I prayed over the rape and the little gay boy hiding and trying to please his family and everyone else so they would just love him. I'll never understand the rape and its meaning in my life, but I do know it happened. And I realize it made me a victim. Maybe it taught me to close the closet door so tight no light would get in, and then to lock it, bolt it, and brick it up so I could hide in a darkness so deep and so black that I would never have a chance of seeing the light, or myself, again – even in the face of real love.

I do not understand why I hid being gay for so long. I prayed to be at peace with my long history of hiding. I prayed to let it go, to let it be.

I prayed for my family. I forgave Marco for his bullying and my parents for somehow allowing it to happen. I forgave everyone in my family for any hurt and pain they ever caused me, and I prayed they, in turn, would forgive me any pain I may have ever caused them. I wish them well and I let them go. I let them be.

I prayed for my childhood friend, Jeff - the friend I called a queer and deserted, because I knew what was obviously in him was also hidden in me. I pray he forgives me. I wish him well and I let him go. I let him be.

I prayed for Jacob and Wendy. I prayed they would forgive me the wrongs I did them as I forgive them the wrongs they did me. I wish them well and I let them go. I let them be.

Furthermore, I bless Wendy for giving me one of the greatest gift life has given me, my daughter Cynthia.

I prayed for Jennifer and begged God to forgive us for the wrongs we did each other. May Jennifer find it in her heart to forgive me as I forgive her. I wish her well and I let her go. I let her be.

I prayed for Marty and Alberto. They showed me what love was but I wasn't ready. I do pray they have forgiven me for the pain I know I caused them. With no regrets but with loving acceptance of my journey in life, I wish them well and I let them go. I let them be.

I prayed for Bradley. I forgave him his abuse of me. I blessed him for finally making me come out to my family. I pray he forgives me for any harm I did him. I wish him well and I let him go. I let him be.

I prayed for the blessings of Rico and Tyrone in my life, and, as I did, I felt Tyrone's presence with me. I prayed for all my friends and felt the light of the love of my friends in my life.

Then I prayed for Greg and as I did I found myself thanking God for the gift of Greg in my life, for the gift of me, myself, finally in another person's life, in Greg's life.

I prayed that anyone I hurt in my hiding would forgive me as I now forgave them and the harm they may have done to me. Most of all, I forgive myself and place the hurt and the pain of it in God's hands and I let it go. I let it be.

Finally, I prayed for everyone who has ever been vulnerable enough to be abused, bullied, or otherwise violated by another person, particularly a member of their own family. We're given this gift of life to love one another, and I pray that some day we will – just love one another.

I am me.

Acknowledgments

Bob Redman, my best friend and my mentor gave me the courage to confront my life and to write this book.

My daughter, my greatest gift from God.

Greg, my life partner, who showed me that I could really find true love. He promised that no one will ever hurt me again. I love you with all my heart honey.

Mike Cismesia, for your talented contribution of promotional material and website development.

Adeline Sides, my photographer and book cover designer, did an amazing job of capturing my determination to be a survivor and a role model.

James Sandrolini, my technical writer who captured the essence of fear that paralyses a victim, and the will power that defines a survivor.

To my wonderful friends and relatives; Tom & Liz Wolfe, Doniece Wall, Lisa Day, and Monica Gadzinowski thank you for your unwavering support.

Mom and Dad you did all you could to protect me and I miss and love you may your rest in peace.

Dedication

To everyone who has been a victim of sexual abuse, rape, molestation, and bullying may you find the courage to stand up and reclaim your life!

About the Author

Patrick Dati has broken his silence telling the world about the abuse and bullying he endured throughout his childhood and adult life. This memoir is also a tortuous coming out story of a man raised in the midst of a devout Catholic family whose members he loved and spent years trying to please by reliving their dreams for him. He attempted suicide twice, and found freedom and himself one day in three simple words: "I have survived."

In living to please others, Patrick married twice and today is the proud father of a beautiful and loving teenage daughter. Recently, he met a man he loves and is now sharing his life with his partner. Because of the life he lived, Patrick is now a public speaker and advocate for several organizations devoted to preventing childhood abuse and bullying.

CPSIA information can be obtained at www.ICGtesting.com
Printed in the USA
LVOW06s1806090414

381019LV00006B/852/P